Albino Luciani

Illustrissimi

The Letters of
Pope John Paul I

Preface by Cardinal Hume
Translated by Isabel Quigly
Illustrated by Papas

COLLINS
Fount Paperbacks

First published in Italy in 1976 by Grafiche
del Messagero di S. Antonio, Padua

First published in the English translation by
William Collins Sons & Co. Ltd.,
London, 1978

First issued in Fount Paperbacks, 1979

Made and printed in Great Britain by
William Collins Sons & Co. Ltd., Glasgow

Illustrissimi

Albino Luciani was born in 1912 in the small village of Forni di Canale (now known as Canale d'Agordo), situated between Venice and the Italian border with Austria.

He studied at the seminary of Belluno, was ordained in 1935, and was then sent to the Gregorian University in Rome where he took a degree in theology. After several years teaching theology at the Belluno seminary, Luciani was appointed Vicar General of Belluno in 1948, and ten years later Pope John XXIII, who thought very highly of him, named him Bishop of Vittorio Veneto. In 1969 he became Patriarch of Venice, and on 5 March 1973 Pope Paul VI made him a cardinal.

On the death of Pope Paul, Albino Luciani was elected Pope on 26 August 1978, taking the name John Paul in honour of his two immediate predecessors.

After only 33 days in office, Pope John Paul I died of a heart attack during the evening of 28 September 1978

CONTENTS

Preface

When I agreed to write the Preface to the English edition of the 'Letters' written by Pope John Paul I when he was Patriarch of Venice, I little thought that before I had completed the task we would be mourning his death. This totally unexpected loss, and the sorrow it brought to millions of people throughout the world, naturally means that I now approach this task with very different thoughts and ideas from those in my mind when I accepted the publisher's invitation in mid-September.

During his thirty-three days' ministry, Pope John Paul I endeared himself to people, both in his few televised appearances, in his audiences and in his words recorded in the press. But part, at least, of the world-wide sorrow his untimely death aroused, came, I think, from a sense of personal deprivation that we had not had more time to get to know and appreciate him. People are left with unanswered questions about this Pope who, in the words of the funeral oration 'passed like a meteor which unexpectedly lights up the heavens and then disappears, leaving us amazed and astonished'.

This is why I am particularly pleased that his 'Letters' to 'Illustrissimi' are being made available to an English-speaking public, and I am happy to introduce them. Other Popes wrote encyclicals. Good Pope John XXIII wrote diaries, too. But, as Pope, John Paul I wrote little and so we must turn to his writings whilst Patriarch of Venice to obtain further insight into the man, his thoughts and his ideals.

The 'Letters' published here are not private correspondence with his relatives, friends or contemporaries, but are 'open letters' originally printed in the Italian Christian paper *Il Messaggero di Sant'Antonio*, and addressed to various individuals, some fictional, some historical. He writes to legendary figures, to important scientific, historical and literary people, to characters from their books, plays, operas and poems, to saints, and even to Christ himself.

If the recipients are varied, the subjects he discusses with them are even more so. There is scarcely a modern problem which he does not mention: from the increasing numbers of 'unemployed intellectuals', to the press; from tourism to the sanctity of life.

Although addressed to so many different characters, and related directly to their particular interests, these letters of Albino Luciani are really meant for you and for me, for the ordinary person living in the 1970s. He wrote them as a teaching device, as a means of proclaiming the Gospel, of opening people's minds and hearts anew to the message of Christianity. Naturally, since they were originally written for an Italian readership, many of the characters addressed are Italian. Some of the examples used are not those that an English writer would employ. Nevertheless, what he says is intended for everyone and will speak to those who read these pages with an open mind.

Then, too, these letters do reveal the writer. Albino Luciani, Cardinal Patriarch of Venice, is revealed in this book as a man rooted in the Gospel, but with his feet firmly on twentieth-century ground and with his eyes twinkling as he calmly surveyed the contemporary, tempestuous, troubled world, smiling at its absurdities, regretting its evil, rejoicing in its good. A man firm in his faith in God, in his hope, and in his love for all the children of the Father, wayward or docile. Humorous when he muses on the follies and frivolities of people, he is firm in maintaining Christian ethics and moral standards. A consummate teacher, widely read, a born raconteur with a fund of anecdotes and illustrations at his command, a man who understood people from within, who identified with them, yet a man to whom his faith was the breath of life and the source of joy.

This writer is indeed the same smiling man whom we began to know as Pope John Paul I. The man who called children to talk with him during papal audiences, who deftly turned their unexpected replies to good account in developing the point he wanted to make, who delighted the crowds with his stories. He is here within the covers of this book. I hope it will be read and re-read. I have no doubt at all that it will be.

BASIL HUME
October 1978   Archbishop of Westminster

Foreword*

Writing to Charles Dickens, in one of his letters in the popular Christian paper the *Messaggero di S. Antonio* collected here, the author says:

'Dear Dickens, I am a bishop who has been given the odd task of writing a letter to some eminent person every month . . .'

Other letters go to Marconi, Marlowe, St Bernardine of Siena, Penelope and Pinocchio, and to all kinds of other characters, historical and mythical, from all sorts of places and periods.

The bishop is Cardinal Albino Luciani, Patriarch of Venice.

You might expect letters from a patriarch to be stuffy and official documents on Church matters, far removed from the lives of ordinary people. Whereas these are written in a lively, journalistic prose that is highly amusing (as well as spiritual), and belongs entirely to everyday life. The letters are concerned with contemporary problems affecting all kinds of people. Cardinal Luciani has had an unusually direct experience of everyday life and expresses himself in a chatty, simple way, dealing with some of the less obvious aspects of people in high places, of working men and women, of students and the old. In a highly unstarchy way he looks at bodies and souls, the human and the divine, without prejudice and with great tolerance. He uses surprisingly sharp arguments, funny stories, and amusing anecdotes that have an English style of humour—helped by his wide knowledge of English literature—as well as a direct knowledge of the minds of ordinary people. The reader may burst out laughing, and will want to read on from sheer joy; he will want to go more deeply into the subjects dealt with, yet will do so without strain, and will above all be persuaded by the examples used.

*This Foreword was written for the original Italian edition of *Illustrissimi*, first published in 1976 when Pope John Paul I was Patriarch of Venice.

The open-minded reader will see the relevance of Christianity to the world today, and realize that without it society will fall to pieces—unless God holds it together.

Today's theories of the 'death of God' and the abolition of the devil (about whom Luciani agrees with Baudelaire that 'The devil's most successful trick is to make men believe that he does not exist'), mean that the old language of Christian apologetics has been lost. But in these living letters, with their amazing modernity, a powerful new language is born, one that is cheerful and straightforward, free of learned quotations and full of events from everyday life. This is a language in which matters of life and death, suffering and evil, are applied to our own times. And, in the light of eternal wisdom, we find a defence of the individual and of society, which so many are doing their best to bring down.

The cardinal thus comes down from his throne and goes in among the people, sharing their everyday life; and, while answering the call of the Second Vatican Council, he revives the attitudes of Christ himself. Peter asked his master to stay up on the heights of Mount Tabor, in static ecstasy, but Jesus went down among the crowds at once, showing them how to live and curing their physical and moral ills. And he did it out of pure love, which is the basis of this new presentation of the 'good news'.

It is this kind of love that makes the author involve himself in everything that affects people personally or socially. Understanding and critical, up-to-date and learned, he discovers mysterious cases of faith in God, with all its beauty and its reality, in quite ordinary problems. Thus he infuses material things with a touch of spirituality, and deflates the exaggerated ideas of various circles—sociological or political.

This is a new kind of teaching, attractive and persuasive and addressed to everyone, the learned and the simple, those near to him and far away; just as earth, air and water, the heavens and religion itself, are made for everyone.

The author of these letters always appears free (free from evil, that is, of course), understanding and patient. 'You launched a crusade,' he writes to St Bernard of Clairvaux: 'something that is argued about a great deal today, but in those days was a part of life.'

He addresses the common man, and sees himself as an example of one; and, just as he admits his own limitations, so he speaks out clearly and tells the truth. Without ever being the least bit offensive, he persuades the most reluctant to see reason, for their own good. There are no enemies in his writings, only brothers; brothers who have a right to be informed, and often enlightened.

His teaching, I repeat, applies to everyone, professional people and workers, the good and the bad, clergy and laity, bishops and fathers of families. He is the first to profit from it himself; it is, after all, teaching men to live well and die well. He seems to feel that politicians, administrators and officials, businessmen and workmen, students and young girls—in other words, all of us—have something to say, are relevant to his teaching. And he always ends by reminding us that we are all children of the same Father.

And so his teaching helps to educate the people whose customs and ways of life he looks at. He combines these sociological attitudes with a lighthearted but penetrating tilt at those who have used the freedom God gave them to make themselves enemies of God in heaven and of men on earth. He links what is divine and what is human, as the Council urged should be done, and thus keeps removing the poison from human life. Even the least attentive non-believer can understand him.

For this reason he deals with the most varied subjects: faith and education, holiness and culture, sex and marriage, tourism and mysticism . . . and, wherever possible, suggests remedies as well as saying what is wrong. He follows the tradition of those who were great moulders of souls—Philip Neri, Bernardine of Siena, Francis de Sales, Pope John. He always speaks clearly and concisely, showing us the present-day life of a bishop who has not cut himself off from the world but lives in it, helping people through the complexities of life. And so he translates his own optimism, which is firmly rooted in Christ, into an original, fresh, exultant joyfulness that is immensely valuable in a world where we are overwhelmed by so many cloudy, self-regarding, overweening attitudes.

Cardinal Luciani is against dreariness, a friend of joy. His ideas are inspired by the Gospels and the Church, and he believes in the universal nature of a Christian's duties. This universality means that he is open to the whole of the rational world, both within Christianity and outside it, rather as St Justin the martyr was; it also means that he gathers up and uses people and ideas from systems other than his own.

Like Terence, he considers nothing human is alien to himself. This is the position from which human unity, the result of the politics of love, can be achieved.

In teaching Christ's testament of love, Cardinal Luciani adds a 'practical' love that consists of faith and works, through a modest, bit-by-bit form of charity which involves forgiving violence or error, endlessly, wherever it comes from.

In any other case, I should have been embarrassed to give unreserved praise to an author. But I am not at all embarrassed to give it to the Patriarch of Venice, since in these letters he has dealt most amusingly and dismissively with praises and compliments. It is years since I had so attractive and lively a book in my hands, or one so useful to me and, I believe, to anyone else.

Igino Giordani

The Letters

CHARLES DICKENS, English author (1812–70). A harsh childhood (his father
was imprisoned for debt and he began work in a factory at the age of ten)
inspired his best-known novels (*David Copperfield, Oliver Twist*), although all his
works are equally celebrated for their humour (*The Pickwick Papers*). The
very effective realism of his work, full of warmth and humanity, had a strong
influence on the reform of English law dealing with children.

To Charles Dickens

Dear Dickens,
I am a bishop who has been given the odd task of writing a letter to some eminent person every month for the *Messaggero di S. Antonio*.

I was pushed for time, around Christmas, and didn't know whom to choose. And then I saw an advertisement in a newspaper for your famous Christmas books and thought to myself; 'I'll write to him. I read his books as a boy, and really loved them; they were filled with love for the poor and a sense of the need for social reform, they were warm and imaginative and human'. So here I am, bothering you.

* * *

First of all I remembered your love for the poor. You felt it and expressed it splendidly, because, as a child, you lived among the poor.

When you were ten you went to work in a factory. Your father was in prison for debt, and to help your mother and the younger children you worked from morning till night in a workshop that made blacking for cleaning shoes, watched by a stern master. At night you slept in an attic. Sundays were spent with the whole family in prison, to keep your father company, and there your young eyes were opened wide and took in all sorts of sad sights, feeling pity, and noting everything.

This is why your novels are filled with poor people, who live in shocking conditions: women and children working in factories or shops, children even younger than seven: no trade union to protect them; no protection against illness and misfortune, either; starvation wages; work that goes on for as much as fifteen hours a day, and frail people tied to the ghastly monotony of powerful, roaring machines in physically and morally unhealthy conditions, often pressed to seek forgetfulness in drink or escape into prostitution.

15

These were the oppressed, and on them you poured all your sympathy. Opposite them stood the oppressors, whom you branded with a pen dipped in anger and irony, a pen whose acid point could have cut into bronze.

* * *

One of your characters is Scrooge, the main character in your *Christmas Carol*.

Two gentleman come to visit him in his office. 'At this festive season of the year, Mr Scrooge,' one of them says, 'it is more than usually desirable that we make some slight provision for the poor and destitute, who suffer greatly at the present time.' 'Are there no prisons? . . . And the union workhouses . . . are they still in operation?' asks Scrooge. 'Under the impression that they scarcely furnish Christian cheer of mind or body to the multitude,' says the gentleman, 'a few of us are endeavouring to raise a fund to buy the poor some meat and drink, and means of warmth. . . . What shall I put you down for?' 'Nothing,' answers Scrooge, '. . . I wish to be left alone. Since you ask me what I wish, gentleman, that is my answer. I don't make merry myself at Christmas, and I can't afford to make idle people merry. I help to support the establishments I have mentioned: they cost enough: and those who are badly off must go there.' 'Many can't go there; and many would sooner die.' 'If they would rather die,' says Scrooge, 'they had better do it, and decrease the surplus population. . . . It's not my business. It's enough for a man to understand his own business, and not to interfere with other peoples! Mine occupies me constantly. Good afternoon, gentleman!'

This was how you presented your Scrooge: busy with nothing but money and business. But when he talks to the ghost of his dead partner Marley, he hears the spirit's sad lament: 'Business!' cries the ghost. 'Mankind was my business. The common welfare was my business; charity, mercy, forebearance, and benevolence were all my business. . . . Why did I walk through crowds of fellow-beings with my eyes turned down, and never raise them to that blessed Star which led the Wise

Men to a poor abode! Were there no poor homes to which its light would have conducted *me*!'

* * *

Over a hundred years have gone by since you wrote those words in 1843. You would be curious to know *if* and *how* the poverty and injustice you denounced have been remedied.

Let me tell you at once. In your country and in the industrialized countries of Europe, the workers' position has improved a great deal. Their only strength lay in numbers. And they used it.

The old socialist speakers used to tell a story: the camel was walking through the desert. Its hooves trod on the grains of sand and he said, proudly and triumphantly: 'I'm squashing you, I'm squashing you!'

The grains of sand let themselves be squashed, but the wind, the terrible desert wind, arose. 'Come on, you grains of sand!' it cried. 'Get together, come along with me! We'll punish that beast and bury him in a great heap of sand!'

The workers, who were once like scattered, separate grains of sand, have become a cloud united by the trade unions and the various forms of socialism, which can undeniably claim to have been the main means of promoting their welfare almost everywhere.

Between your day and ours the workers have advanced in every field, achieving their goals economically, in social security, and in cultural matters. Today, through the unions, they often manage to be heard at the highest levels, where they decide their own fate. All this has come about through sacrifices, by overcoming opposition and obstacles.

At first it was illegal for workers to unite in defence of their rights; later it was tolerated that they should, and later still it was recognized by law. In the old days the state was a 'police state', and it decreed that contracts between workers and employers were entirely private. It forbade collective agreements. The employer had a knife up his sleeve, and 'free bargaining' ruled, without check. 'If two employees want a

17

workman, his wages will go up. If two workers are looking for an employer, their wages will drop.' This was the law, it was said, and it would lead automatically to the balance of forces. Whereas in fact it led to abuses of capitalism, which was, and in certain cases still is, a wicked system.

*   *   *

And now what happens? In your day, social injustices were of a single kind: they were suffered by the workers, who could accuse the employers. Today, all sorts of people accuse all sorts of others. Workers in the country say they are much less well paid than workers in industry. Here in Italy, the South is against the North. In Africa, Asia and Latin America, the nations of the Third World are against the rich nations.

But even in the rich nations there are plenty of pockets of poverty and insecurity. Many workers are unemployed or uncertain of their jobs. They are not always protected properly against accidents. Often they feel that they are treated merely as a means of production, not as a central part of it.

Then, too, the frantic rush to grow rich, and the exaggerated, crazy use of unnecessary things, has used up necessities: clean air and pure water, silence, inner peace, rest.

We used to think that oil wells were bottomless. Then suddenly we realized that they were nearly empty. We used to think that when, a long way ahead, oil ran out, we could depend on nuclear energy. But now they tell us that the production of nuclear energy involves the dangers of radioactive waste, which is harmful to man and his environment.

There are many fears and worries. To many, the camel in the desert which must be attacked and buried is now not merely capitalism, but the whole present 'system', which must be overturned through revolution. Others think the overturning process has already begun.

Today's poor Third World, they say, will soon be rich, thanks to the oil wells, which it will develop all for itself. The rich consumer society, having only a dribble of oil, will have to cut down its industries and consumption and go into a recession.

Among all these problems, worries and tensions, your principles, dear Dickens, still apply, widened and adapted; principles which you put forward so warmly, if a little sentimentally: love for the poor, and not so much for the individual poor person as for whole peoples, who, having been rejected, either individually or collectively, drew together and achieved solidarity. Christians, following Christ's example, should without hesitation give them sincere, open-hearted love.

Solidarity: we are a single boat full of people who have now been brought together, but in a stormy sea. If we want to avoid serious clashes, this is the rule: all for one and one for all; press on with what unites us, forget what divides us.

Trust in God: through your character, Marley's Ghost, you said you wished the Wise Men's star would light up the homes of the poor.

Today the whole world is a home of the poor, and in such need of God!

MARK TWAIN (pseudonym of Samuel Langhorne Clemens), American writer and humorist (1835–1910). A printer, a pilot on the Mississippi steamboats and a journalist, he became celebrated as an interpreter of the myth of the new frontier. His masterpieces are the richly humorous *Adventures of Tom Sawyer* and *Adventures of Huckleberry Finn*.

To Mark Twain

Dear Mark Twain,

When I was a boy, you were one of my favourite writers. I still remember *The Adventures of Tom Sawyer*, which were the adventures of your own childhood. Some of your stories I've told people a hundred times—the one about the value of books, for instance. A little girl asked you a question about it, and you told her that books were inestimably valuable, but that their value varied. A leather-bound book was fine for sharpening a razor; a small, concise book—the kind the French write—is wonderfully useful for propping up the shortest table-leg; a big book, like a dictionary, is the best weapon for throwing at cats; and finally, an atlas with large pages contains the very best sort of paper for mending windows.

When I said: 'Now I'm going to tell you another of Mark Twain's stories', my students were always delighted. But I'm afraid people in my diocese are going to be shocked. 'A bishop quoting Mark Twain!' they'll say. Perhaps I ought to explain that bishops vary just as much as books. Some are like eagles, soaring high above us, bearing important messages; others are nightingales, who sing God's praises in a marvellous way; and others are poor wrens, who simply squawk on the lowest branch of the ecclesiastical tree, trying to express the odd thought on some great subject.

Dear Twain, I am one of this latter kind. So I shall simply cheer up and recall that you once said: 'Man is more complex than he seems. Every adult has in him not one but three distinct men.' 'How is that?' you were asked. 'Well, take any man called John. In him there's John the First, that is, the man he thinks he is; there's John the Second, the man others think he is; and finally there's John the Third, the man he really is.'

*   *   *

Now there's a great deal of truth in that story of yours, dear

21

Twain. Take John the First. When we're shown a group photograph in which we've appeared, which is the nice pleasant face we first look for? I hate to say it, but it's our own. Because we like ourselves enormously, we prefer ourselves to other people. As we like ourselves so much, we tend to emphasize our good points and diminish our bad ones, and to have a different scale of values for other people from the one we have for ourselves. And how do we emphasize our good points? Trilussa, a fellow-writer of yours, describes the way we do it: 'Vanity, the snail, had crawled over an obelisk,' he writes. 'She looked back at the slimy track behind her and said: "I see I've left my mark on History".'

That's what we're like, dear Twain: just a touch of slime, so long as it's ours and just because it's ours, is enough to make us feel pleased and proud.

And how do we diminish our faults? 'I take a drop very occasionally,' a man will tell you. Other people will say he's like a sponge, never without his throat parched, his elbow raised. 'I'm a little nervous, I sometimes get upset,' a woman will say. Upset! Other people call her moody, vile-tempered, vengeful, an impossible creature, a harpy!

In Homer, the gods went about the world in a cloud that hid them from the eyes of men. We have a cloud around us that hides us from our own eyes.

Francis de Sales, a bishop like me and a humorist like you, wrote: 'We blame our neighbour for small faults, and forgive ourselves for big ones. We try to sell things at a high price, yet wish to buy them at a bargain. We want justice for other people, but mercy for ourselves. We want what we say to be taken generously, yet we're stuffy over what others say. If one of our inferiors is rude to us, we dislike whatever he does; whereas if we like someone, we forgive him anything, whatever he does. We demand our rights strictly, but want others to be moderate in claiming theirs . . . What we do for others seems a great deal to us, what others do for us seems nothing at all.'

*　　*　　*

That's enough of John the First. Let's have a look at John the Second. I think there are two things here, dear Twain: this John either wants people to admire him, or else he's upset because people ignore and undervalue him. Nothing wrong with that; but we must try not to exaggerate in either case. 'Woe unto you,' said our Lord, 'if you take the best seats in the synagogue and people bow to you in the market place . . . and if you do everything in order to be noticed.' Today he would say: 'If you achieve success and honours by elbowing others out of the way, by patronage, by doing all you can to get into the papers.'

But why 'Woe unto you'? When Hitler went through Florence in 1938, the city was covered in swastikas and enthusiastic posters. Bargellini said to Dalla Costa: 'You see, Eminence? You see?' 'Don't worry,' the cardinal replied. 'His fate is set down in Psalm 37: "I have seen the wicked in great power, and spreading himself like a green bay tree. Yet he passed away and lo, he was not: yea, I sought him, and he could not be found."'

Sometimes that 'woe' doesn't mean divine punishment but human ridicule. A man may be like the ass that wore the lion's skin, so that everyone cried: 'Look out, mind the lion!' and men and beasts fled before him. But the wind blew, and the skin was lifted off his back, and everyone saw the ass. And people rushed furiously at him, and made him carry a great load of wood.

And suppose the opposite happens? Suppose people think badly of you, what's to be done about that? Here are some more of Christ's words that may help: 'John came, who neither ate nor drank, and they said: He has a devil in him. The Son of Man came, and he ate and drank, and they say: He is a glutton and a drinker, a friend of publicans and sinners.' Even Christ didn't manage to please everyone. So let's not mind too much if we don't, either.

* * *

John the Third was a cook. This isn't one of your stories, Twain, but one of Tolstoy's. The dogs were lying in the kitchen doorway. John killed a calf and threw the offal into the yard. The dogs gobbled it up and said: 'What a good cook!' A little later, John

'Some are like eagles, . . . others are nightingales, . . . and others are poor wrens . . .'

shelled some peas and chopped some onions and threw the pods and skins into the yard. The dogs leapt on them, then turned away. 'The cook's gone off, he's no good now,' they said. John didn't mind in the least what they thought. 'It's my master who's going to eat and appreciate my meals, not the dogs. If he likes them, that's good enough for me.'

Good for Tolstoy, as well. But I wonder: what does Our Lord like? What does he like in us? One day when he was preaching someone told him: 'Your mother and your brethren are outside, and ask to speak to you.' He held his hand out to his disciples and said: 'These are my mother and my brethren. Whoever does the will of my Father, he is my brother, my sister and my mother.'

That is the man he likes: the man who does his will. He likes us to pray to him, but he very much dislikes our making prayer an excuse for neglecting the effort of doing good works. 'Why do you call me Lord, Lord and not do what I say?' he asked. Do what he says, then!

This may sound like a moralizing way to end. As a humorist, dear Twain, you wouldn't have drawn this conclusion. But as I'm a bishop I'm bound to draw it, and to tell my people: 'If you happen to remember the three Johns (or the three Jameses or Toms) who are found in each one of us, then remember the third in particular: the one God likes!'

G. K. CHESTERTON, English journalist and author (1874-1936), who
was converted to Catholicism in 1922. He wrote many novels and was a
brilliant polemicist, who longed for an ideal society without social
inequalities, based on good sense, religion, and humour. His many
books included *The Napoleon of Notting Hill, The Man Who Was Thursday,*
and the Father Brown stories.

To G. K. Chesterton

Dear Chesterton,

On Italian television during the past few weeks we have been seeing Father Brown, your surprising detective-priest—a character who is typically yours. A pity we haven't also had Professor Lucifer and the monk Michael. I'd very much have liked to see them as you described them in *The Ball and the Cross*, sitting beside each other on the flying ship.

When the flying ship is above St Paul's Cathedral, the Professor gives 'a shriek indescribable' as they pass the cross on the ball set on top of the dome.

'"I once knew a man like you, Lucifer,"' says Michael. '"... This man also took the view that the symbol of Christianity was a symbol of savagery and all unreason. His history is rather amusing. It is also a perfect allegory of what happens to rationalists like yourself. He began, of course, by refusing to allow a crucifix in his house, or round his wife's neck, or even in a picture. He said, as you say, that it was an arbitrary and fantastic shape, that it was a monstrosity, loved because it was paradoxical. Then he began to grow fiercer and more eccentric; he would batter the crosses by the roadside; for he lived in a Roman Catholic country. Finally in a height of frenzy he climbed the steeple of the Parish Church and tore down the cross, waving it in the air, and uttering wild soliloquies up there under the stars. Then one still summer evening as he was wending his way homewards, along a lane, the devil of his madness came upon him with a violence and transfiguration which changes the world. He was standing smoking, for a moment, in front of an interminable line of palings, when his eyes were opened. Not a light shifted, not a leaf stirred, but he saw as if by a sudden change in the eyesight that this paling was an army of innumerable crosses linked together over hill and dale. And he whirled up his heavy stick and went at it as if at an army. Mile after mile along his homeward path he broke it down and tore it up. For he hated the cross and every paling is a wall of crosses. When he returned to his house he was a literal madman. He sat upon a chair and then started up from it for the crossbars of the carpentry repeated the intolerable image. He flung himself upon a bed only to remember that this, too, like all workmanlike things, was constructed on the accursed plan. He broke his furniture because it was made of crosses. He burnt his house because it was made of crosses. He was found in the river." '

'Lucifer was looking at him with a bitten lip,' you continue. ' "Is that story really true?" he asked.

"Oh, no," said Michael, airily. "It is a parable. It is a parable of you and all your rationalists. You begin by breaking up the Cross; but you end by breaking up the habitable world." '

The monk's conclusion, which is yours, dear Chesterton, is quite right. Take God away and what is left, what do men become? What sort of a world are we reduced to living in? 'Why, the world of progress!' I hear someone say. 'The world of affluence!' Yes, but this famous progress isn't all it was once cracked up to be. It contains other things in itself: missiles, bacteriological and atomic weapons, the present process of pollution—all things that, unless they are dealt with in time, threaten to plunge the whole human race into catastrophe.

In other words, progress that involves men who love one another, thinking of themselves as brothers and as children of the one Father, God, can be a magnificent thing. Progress that involves men who don't recognize a single Father in God becomes a constant danger: without a parallel moral progress, which is continuous and internal, it develops what is lowest and cruellest in man, making him a machine possessed by machines, a number manipulated by numbers; he becomes what Papini called 'a raving savage, who, to satisfy his predatory, destructive, and licentious instincts, no longer uses a club, but has the immense forces of nature and mechanical invention to draw upon.'

Yes, I know there are plenty of people who think the opposite of this. They consider religion a consoling dream, invented by oppressed people who imagine another world, a non-existent world in which they can later find what is stolen from them today by their oppressors. These oppressors have arranged the whole thing for their own benefit, to keep the oppressed underfoot and to quieten the instinct towards a class struggle, an instinct that, were it not for religion, would urge them to fight.

It is no good reminding these people that the Christian religion itself favours the revival of proletarian awareness, that it exalts the poor and foresees a just future. 'Yes,' they reply, 'Christianity does awaken the awareness of the poor, but then it paralyses it by preaching patience, and by substituting faith in God and trust in the gradual reform of society for the class struggle.'

Many also think that God and religion, by fixing people's hopes and efforts on a future, distant paradise, *alienate* man, and prevent him committing himself to a nearby paradise, to achieving one here on earth.

It is no good reminding them that, according to the recent Council, a Christian, just because he is a Christian, must feel all the more committed to support progress for the good of all, and social advancement for everyone. 'All the same,' they say, 'you think of progress through a transitory world, waiting for a definitive paradise which will never be achieved. We want our paradise here, as a result of all our struggles. We can see the beginning of it already, whereas your God is actually called "dead" by some theologians. We agree with Heine, who wrote: "Do you hear the bells? Down on your knees! We are taking the last sacraments to a dying God."'

Dear Chesterton, you and I go down on our knees before a God who is more present than ever. Only he can give a satisfactory answer to the questions which, for everyone, are the most important of all: Who am I? Where did I come from? Where am I going?

As to the heaven that will be enjoyed on earth and only on earth, and in the near future, after the famous 'class struggle', I'd like to quote someone much more gifted than me and, without denying your merits, than you too, dear Chesterton: Dostoevsky.

You remember his Ivan Karamazov. He was an atheist, a

friend of the devil. Well, he protested with all an atheist's vehemence against the paradise achieved through effort, suffering, and the martyrdom of countless generations. To think of our descendants being happy thanks to the unhappiness of their ancestors! Ancestors who struggle without ever receiving their share of joy, often without even the comfort of a glimpse of paradise when they emerge from the hell they have gone through!

30

such nonsense on her head.'

a woman's beauty stands out without any need

*   *   *

would you believe it? There is a colleague of
who seems even more understanding than you.
les was amused and indulgent at all the small
uman weaknesses that make people, especially
anging their ornaments, their appearance and
nd was particularly indulgent towards the
ce of young ladies. 'These,' he wrote, 'feel
d to please others.' And he goes on: 'It is
r them to wish to please many, although they
: intention of catching one, in marriage.'
i he was, it was he who had to moderate the
ss de Chantal, who was too austere about her
s: 'Well, little girls should be pretty; you
need be he could gently reproach the small
s they were really small!) acts of boldness in
mily. One day, when Françoise de Rabutin
m wearing a rather low-cut dress, he smilingly
ins.

e same moderation over matters of fashion
narried women. Madame Charmoisy had a
as worried because all his friends were 'so
ed than he was'. This was not right, the
ise 'since we live in the world, we must
the world in all that is not sin'. Madame
ad a worry: could she—devout as she was—
according to the fashion? 'Oh heavens!'
ahead and powder it boldly! Even pheasants

things like these, Francis de Sales thought
ensible Christian advice, leaving the devout
their thorns. Yet they were badly received,
great Bossuet wrote that, with his advice,

Multitudes exterminated, wounded and sacrificed merely to provide the soil in which to grow the future trees of life! Impossible! says Ivan. It would be a pitiless, monstrous injustice.

And he was right.

The sense of justice that lies in every man, whatever his faith, demands that the good we do and the evil we suffer should be rewarded, that the hunger for life found in everyone should be satisfied. Where and how, if there is no other life? And from whom, if not from God? And from what God, if not the one of whom St Francis de Sales wrote: 'Do not fear God, who wishes you no harm, but love him a great deal, who wishes you so much good.'

What many people fight is not the true God but the false idea they have made of God: a God who protects the rich, who only asks and demands, who is jealous of our growing prosperity, who spies continuously on our sins from above, to give himself the pleasure of punishing us.

Dear Chesterton, you know God isn't like that; you know that he's both good and just; the father of prodigal sons, who wishes them all to be, not sad and wretched, but great and free, and creators of their own destiny. Our God is not man's rival, he wants us to be his friends, he has called us to share in his divine nature and in his eternal happiness. And he does not ask anything excessive of us: he is content with very little, because he knows quite well that we haven't got very much.

Dear Chesterton, I'm sure, as you are, that this God will make himself ever more known and loved: by everyone, including those who reject him, not because they are evil (they may be better than both of us!), but because they look at him from a mistaken point of view. If they continue not to believe in him, he replies: 'Well, I believe in you!'

MARIA THERESA OF AUSTRIA (1717–80), wife of Francis I and Empress of the Hapsburg dominions from 1740. An 'enlightened' ruler, she governed in a paternalistic way, and was an exemplary wife and mother. She wrote some letters which have survived, to her daughter, the unfortunate Marie Antoinette, about her style of dressing.

To the Em

Imperial Ma
I know you only fror
of the age of enlightenm
paternalistic way. Your
your domain, but it w
be obedient children of

There's nothing sur
look cannot be expecte
the rulers of your age
You conducted the st
the instruments!

As a wife and mo
was loved and since
you knew he had be
lived in what might
subjects could gaze
You had sixteen chi
called the 'Sacrista
Prussia, and the u
then Queen of Fran

It was to her
survive, on the subj
both as a woman a

It was rumoure
her appearance.
immediately wrot
badly, and that y

When she be
the other way,
monumental hea
at least ten metr
feel,' you said,
Fashion should

I.—B

Queen needs n
How wise:
for 'nonsense'.

Your Majesty,
mine, a bishop,
St Francis de Sa
but tenacious h
women, keep ch
their clothes; a
flirtatious elegar
innately the nee
perfectly right fo
do it with the sol

Bishop thoug
zeal of the Baron
daughters' clothe
know.' But when
(and in those day
the girls of his fa
appeared before h
offered her some

He showed th
among men and r
young son who w
much better dress
saint wrote, becau
follow the laws of
le Blanc de Mions
powder her hair
replied Francis, 'go
preen themselves!'

When he wrote
that he was giving s
life its roses but not
your Majesty. The

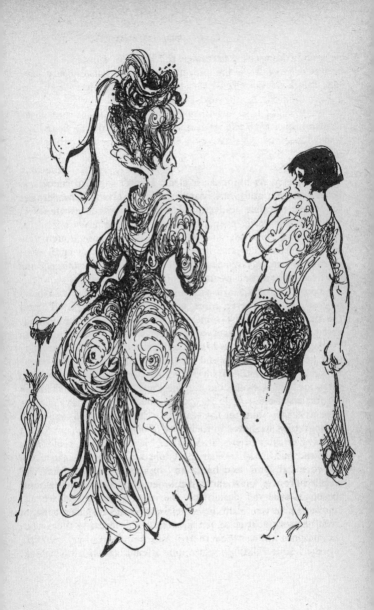

he merely 'put cushions under the knees of sinners'. A friar actually spoke from the pulpit against his *Introduction to the Devout Life*, the book in which St Francis had written the things I have quoted. At the end of his sermon he had a lighted candle brought to him with great solemnity, pulled the book out from his sleeve and set it alight, scattering the ashes to the four winds.

* * *

Your Majesty, let me make it clear, I don't support this friar! I am with you and with Francis de Sales, taking a moderate, proper stand that understands and encourages all that is healthily attractive, even in fashion. But I am with you in condemning nonsense. And what a lot of nonsense there is in our day! In clothes and in what is obviously connected with them: expense, ways of behaving, entertainment! Not to mention the beaches and the way some people behave on them.

Your daughter Marie Antoinette had ten metres of fabric on her head and even more in her dress and train. Today the opposite happens: some women wear scarcely anything and go about like that everywhere, even trying to enter churches.

At your court Pietro Metastasio wrote melodramas, among your gentlemen in wigs and powdered ladies. In one of them he said: 'The faith of lovers is like the Arabian phoenix: everyone says it exists, but no one knows where it is.' This is the furthest he dared go in writing about love. Today, people dare to do anything in the way they dress, sing and write, in photography, in shows, in their way of behaving.

In your day, here in Venice, Margherita in Goldoni's *Campiello* said: 'My mother used to take me to the opera, or else to the theatre, and had a key to a box. She saw that we went where she knew there would be good plays, and where she could take her daughters; she came with us and we all enjoyed ourselves. Sometimes we went to the Ridotto: a little to the Liston, a little to the Piazzetta, the fortune-tellers and the puppets. When we were at home, we always had our talk together. Our relations came, our friends came, and even a young man now and then; but there was no danger.'

And how are things today? Even in respectable families, girls stay away from home for days on end. Where do they go? With their 'boyfriends', alone in hotels, alone in cars, wandering about the world. Sometimes this happens: an invitation comes for a dance with the initials NET on it—meaning 'No extra trouble', in other words, no parents.

The newspapers tell us that the rhythm and quality of production slows down quite noticeably in some firms because the employees are too busy staring at the skirts or the tiny shorts of the girls they work with. Or else we read that in order to prevent an increase in street accidents, the government is putting up posters warning motorists against being distracted by girls in mini-skirts seen through the windscreen or the windows.

* * *

Your Majesty, you wrote quite truly that a woman needs very little in order to please others. All you need to know is which people you want to please, and what your object is in doing so. Do you want to please everyone? This is not bad in itself, but it may be bad to want to please *in that particular way*. I think a woman should try to please her parents, her brothers and sisters, and, above all, her husband, the man who will choose her as a wife and will be the father of her children.

Now, all these people want a woman to be smart and attractive, but in a context of modesty that makes her even more attractive, as well as morally delightful.

* * *

Your Majesty, forgive me for having confided in you, who approve of these ideas, and for venting my feelings like this. Let me make it clear, it isn't that no women appreciate these ideas today, but that some women think them old-fashioned and out of date. You know that they're still going strong and are always fresh, because they reflect the thoughts of God, who wrote, through St Paul, 'Let women adorn themselves in modest apparel, with shamefacedness and sobriety'.

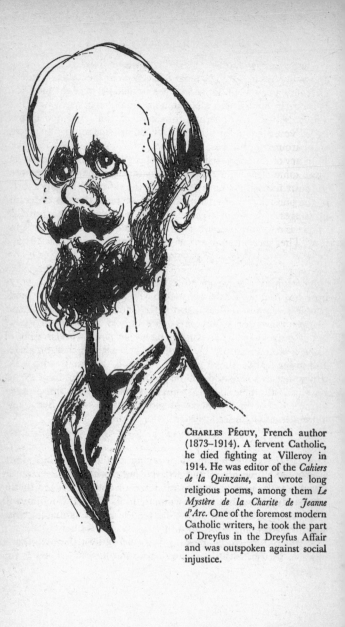

CHARLES PÉGUY, French author (1873–1914). A fervent Catholic, he died fighting at Villeroy in 1914. He was editor of the *Cahiers de la Quinzaine*, and wrote long religious poems, among them *Le Mystère de la Charite de Jeanne d'Arc*. One of the foremost modern Catholic writers, he took the part of Dreyfus in the Dreyfus Affair and was outspoken against social injustice.

To Charles Péguy

Dear Péguy,

I've always liked your enthusiastic spirit, and your passion for arousing and leading souls. But I like rather less your literary outbursts, which are sometimes bitter, sometimes ironic, and sometimes too ardent in the fight against the mistaken men of your time.

Your religious writings contain some poetically successful passages (this is not to say that they are religiously successful). Here is one in which you have God talking of hope.

'The faith of men does not surprise me, God says, it is not a surprising thing: in my creation I am so dazzling that these poor people would have to be blind in order not to see me. The charity of men does not surprise me, says God, it is not a surprising thing; these poor people are so unhappy that unless they had a heart of stone they could not help loving one another. Hope—that is what surprises me!'

I agree with you, dear Péguy, that hope is surprising. I agree with Dante that it means *waiting in certainty*. I agree with what the Bible says about those who hope.

Abraham didn't know why God had ordered him to kill his only child; he didn't see from where the many descendants he had been promised would come, if Isaac were dead, and yet he waited with certainty.

David, going towards Goliath, knew perfectly well that five pebbles, even when flung by someone as expert as he was with the sling, were not enough in the face of an iron-clad giant. And yet he waited with certainty and told the huge man in armour: 'I come to thee in the name of the Lord of hosts, the God of the armies of Israel, whom thou hast defied. This day will the Lord deliver thee into mine hand; and I will smite thee, and take thine head from thee.'

Praying with the Psalms, I also feel transformed into a man who waits with certainty, dear Péguy. 'The Lord is my light and my salvation; whom shall I fear? . . . Though an host should encamp against me, my heart shall not fear: though war should rise against me, in this shall I be confident.'

*   *   *

How wrong are those who do not hope, dear Péguy! Judas was terribly wrong the day he sold Christ for thirty pieces of silver, but he was much more wrong when he thought his sin too great to be forgiven. No sin is too great: a finite wretchedness, however enormous, can always be covered by an infinite mercy.

And it is never too late: God calls himself not only Father, but Father of the prodigal son. He sees us when we are still far away, he is moved, and runs to us, throwing his arms around our neck and kissing us tenderly.

The fact that we may have had a stormy past should not frighten us. Storms that were bad in the past become good in the present if they encourage us to reform and to change; they become jewels if they are given to God, so that he may have the consolation of forgiving them.

The Gospel records four women among Christ's ancestors, three of them not entirely commendable: Rehab was a courtesan; Tamar bore a son, Perez, by her father-in-law Judah; and Bathsheba committed adultery with David. With mysterious humility Christ accepted these relations into his family, but also, I believe, into the hand of God, as a way of saying to us: you may become saints, whatever your family history, your temperament, your heredity and your past.

Dear Péguy, it would be wrong to wait and keep putting things off continually. 'Later' is very often another way of saying 'Never'. I know some people who seem to make life into a perpetual station waiting-room. The trains come and go and they say: 'I'll leave another time! I'll confess at the end of my life!' Visconti-Venosta used to say of 'brave Anselmo': 'A day goes by and then another, but brave Anselmo never returns.' Here we have the opposite: an Anselmo who *never leaves*. It is a risky business. Just suppose, dear Péguy, that the Chinese were invading Italy, advancing, destroying and killing.

Everyone would run away: aeroplanes, cars and trains would be seized. 'Come along!' I'd shout to Anselmo, 'there's still room on the train, get on quickly!' 'Are you really sure the Chinese will kill me, if I stay here?' he'd reply. 'Well, I'm not absolutely sure, they might just spare you, and before they come another train might just go by, but these are outside chances and it's a matter of life and death. It would be crazily risky to wait!'

'Can't I be converted later?' 'Of course, but it may be harder than it will be now. Repeated sins become a habit, they become chains that are harder to break. Do it now, at once, I beg you!'

* * *

You know this, Péguy. Waiting is based on the goodness of God, which appears especially in the behaviour of Christ, who in the Gospel was called the friend of sinners. The extent of this friendship is well known: when he has lost a sheep, our Lord goes looking for it until he finds it: having found it, he puts it happily onto his shoulders, carries it home, and says to everyone: 'Joy shall be in heaven over one sinner that repenteth, more than over ninety and nine just persons, which need no repentance.'

The Samaritan woman, the woman taken in adultery, Zaccheus, the thief crucified on his right, the paralytic and we ourselves, have been sought, found and treated like that. There's another astonishing thing!

* * *

And there's another one again: the waiting with certainty for future glory, as Dante put it. What is surprising is *certainty* set in the *future*, that is, in a dim distance. And yet this, Péguy, is the situation of those of us who hope.

We are like Abraham, who, having been promised a very fertile country by God, obeyed and left, the Bible tells us, not knowing where he was going, yet certain and in the hands of God. We are like those John the Evangelist described: 'We are

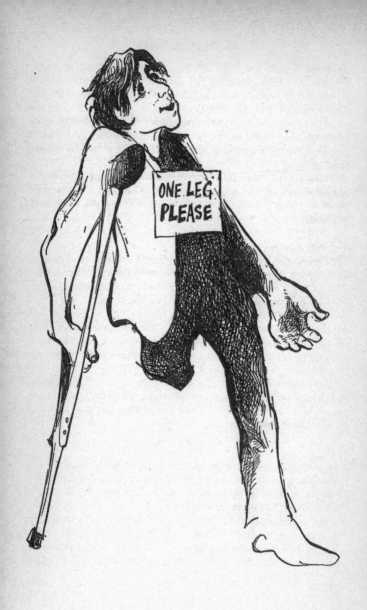

now the sons of God, but what we shall be has not yet been shown.' We find ourselves with Manzoni's Napoleon, 'carried along the flowering paths of hope', even if we have little idea of where the paths will emerge.

Do we know it, at least vaguely? Or was Dante mad when he tried to describe it as light, love and happiness? 'Intellectual light', because our minds up there will see perfectly clearly what down here they have scarcely glimpsed: God. 'Love of true goodness', because the good we love here is a single form of goodness, drops and crumbs and fragments of it, whereas God is *the* good. 'Joy that transcends all pain', because there is no comparison between it and the sweetness of this world.

Augustine agrees when he calls God 'beauty that is always old and always new'. Manzoni agrees: up there 'former glory is silence and darkness'. Isaiah agrees in the famous dialogue: 'The voice said, Cry. And he said, what shall I cry? All flesh is grass, and all the goodliness thereof is as the flower of the field: The grass withereth, the flower fadeth.'

We agree with these great men, dear Péguy. Some may call us 'alienated', poetic and impractical. We shall reply, 'We are the sons of hope, the surprise of God'.

TRILUSSA (pseudonym of Carlo Alberto Salustri), a Roman poet (1871–1950). His satire, which is often informal and good-natured, is also bitingly sarcastic about what he saw as the hypocrisy, cunning and selfishness of the contemporary world. His best-known works are *Fables* (1922) and *Jove and the Animals* (1932).

To Trilussa

Dear Trilussa,

I have re-read the melancholy, autobiographical poem in which you tell us how you were lost in a wood at night, and there met an old blind woman who said: 'If you don't know the way I'll come with you, I know it.' You were surprised: 'It seems strange to me that someone can guide me who cannot see,' you said. But the old woman cut you short, took your hand and said: 'Come along.' That was faith.

I agree with you to some extent: faith is certainly a good guide, a kind, wise old woman who says: put your foot here, take this path up there. But all this happens when faith has already established itself in our minds and become a firm conviction, guiding and directing the action of our lives.

First this conviction must be formed and planted in the mind. And here, dear Trilussa, is our present difficulty. The journey of faith today is not a bewildering walk through a wood, but one that is sometimes difficult, often dramatic and always mysterious.

* * *

It is difficult in the first place to have faith in others, to accept what they say just because they say it. The schoolboy hears his teacher say that the world is 148 million kilometres from the sun. He'd like to check this, but how? He cheers up and holds on to a deliberate act of faith: 'Our teacher is honest and well informed, I'll trust him!'

A mother tells her son about far-off times, and the sacrifices they made to protect him and care for him. 'Do you believe me?' she says. 'Will you remember how much I've done for love of you?' 'How can I fail to believe you?' the son replies. 'I'll do all I can to be worthy of your love.' This son must feel tenderness and love for his mother as well as trust in her; only thus will he know the impulse to self-surrender, the commitment to life.

Faith in God is something like that: it is the 'yes' of a child to its parent, given to God, who tells us something about his own life; it says 'yes' to the things we are told and at the same time to Him who tells them. The man who says 'yes' must have not merely trust but tenderness and love, and must feel like a small child. 'I'm not the sort who knows everything,' he must say, 'the sort who has the last word on everything, who checks everything. I'm used to reaching scientific certainties with the strictest tests in the laboratory; but in this I must be content with a certainty that isn't physical or mathematical, but depends on good sense, on common sense. Not only that, but by trusting myself to God I know I must accept the fact that God may come into my life, and direct it and change it.'

* * *

In his *Confessions*, dear Trilussa, Augustine is much more agitated than you were in describing his journey to faith. Before giving his final 'yes' to God, his soul twisted and turned in the most painful conflicts. On the one hand there was God calling him; on the other, old habits: 'the very toys of toys, and vanities of vanities, my ancient mistresses, still held me,' he writes; 'they plucked my fleshy garment, and whispered softly, "Dost thou cast us off? and from that moment shall we no more be with thee for ever? and from that moment shall not this or that be lawful for thee for ever?"'

God urged him to hasten and Augustine begged: 'Not yet, wait a moment!' and continued for whole weeks in indecision, twisting and turning, until at last, helped by a strong thrust from God, he took his courage in both hands and decided.

As you see, Trilussa, there is a mysterious element in the human drama of faith: the intervention of God. Paul of Tarsus felt it on the road to Damascus and described it thus: 'That day, Lord, you seized me: through your grace I am what I am.'

Here we are at the heart of the mystery. What is the grace of God really, and how does it work? How hard it is to express it!

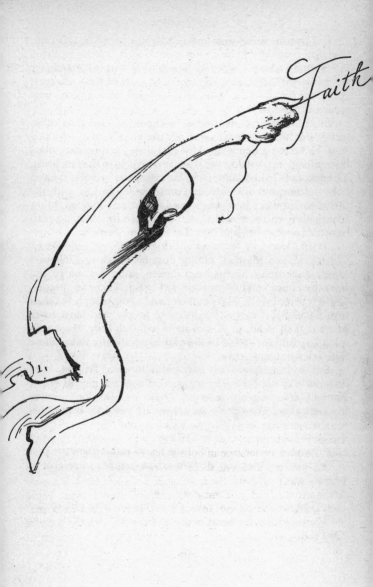

Faith

Imagine the unbeliever is asleep; God wakes him and says: 'Get up!' Imagine that he's a sick man; God puts some medicine in his hand and says: 'Take it.' The truth is that a non-believer suddenly, without having thought of it, finds himself reflecting on the problems of the soul and of religion, and is potentially available to faith.

After this intervention, made 'without us', God does other things, but 'with us', that is, with our free collaboration. Waking us when we are asleep is done by him alone; getting out of bed is something we must do, even if we need his help in the first place. The grace of God has force in it, but refuses to force us; it has a holy violence, but of a kind that makes us fall in love with the truth, not have our freedom violated. What may happen is that having been woken, asked to get up and taken by the arm, a man may turn over in bed and say: 'Let me go on sleeping!'

In the Gospel we see cases of this kind. 'Come, follow me,' Christ said, and Matthew got up from his bench and followed him; another man, having been invited, said: 'Let me go and bury my father,' and never appeared again. There are people, Christ reflected sadly, who put their hand to the plough and then turn back. Belief ranges from that of people who have never had any faith at all, to that of those with too little, those who are lukewarm and feeble in their faith, and finally those whose faith is fervent and active.

But we can explain this only partially, dear Trilussa. Why do some of us not believe? Because God does not give us grace. But why does he not give us grace? Because we don't answer his inspiration. Why don't we answer it? Because, being free, we abuse our freedom. Why do we abuse our freedom? That is the hard thing to say, dear Trilussa, and something I don't understand. I prefer to think of the future rather than the past and follow Paul's invitation: 'We exhort you not to receive in vain the grace of God.'

*   *   *

Dear Trilussa! Manzoni calls the Unnamed's return to the faith a 'glad marvel and a banquet of grace'.* He knew what

* In *The Betrothed*.

he was talking about; he had 'returned' himself.

It is a banquet that is always laid, and one available to us all. Myself, I try to profit from it every day, propping up the life of faith that the previous day's sins have toppled. Perhaps Christians like me, who feel that they are sometimes good and sometimes sinners, will, like me, do their best to be good guests at the banquet.

ST BERNARD OF CLAIRVAUX, saint and Doctor of the Catholic Church (1091–1153), was a monk at Cîteaux, when in 1115 he founded the Cistercian monastery at Clairvaux. He became influential in the papal court of Innocent II and in 1146 he called the Christians in France to the Second Crusade. A mystic, his writings on spiritual subjects had an important influence on Western religion.

To St Bernard, Abbot of Clairvaux

To the Abbot of Clairvaux,

You were a great monk, and in a completely original way a great statesman. There was a time when Clairvaux was more important than Rome: emperors, popes, kings, feudal lords and vassals all came to you. You launched a crusade: something that is argued about a great deal today, but in those days was a part of life.

On the other hand, you were ahead of your time in your opposition to the anti-semitism of the age and in your open defence of the Jews. And you didn't hesitate to speak out. To one of the popes you write: 'What I fear for you is neither sword nor poison, but the pride of power.' And to the King of France, who had appointed an abbot as his army commander, you wrote: 'What will happen now? Will the new general celebrate mass in his helmet and iron greaves, or will he lead the troops in his cotta and stole?'

In the Middle Ages others led Europe with the sword. You did the same with the pen, in letters sent off in all directions, only some of which—about five hundred—have survived.

Most of these discuss ascetic theology. One, however, the twenty-fourth, contains the essence of the Christian vision of government and, in remarkable circumstances, became a classic text.

A conclave to choose a new pope was being held. The cardinals were wavering between three candidates, one outstanding for holiness, one for culture, and the third for practical sense.

One of the cardinals put an end to their indecision by quoting your letter. 'It is no good hesitating any longer,' he said. 'Our case has already been dealt with in the twenty-fourth letter of the Mellifluous Doctor. All we need do is apply it, and everything will go smoothly. So the first candidate is holy? Right, let him pray for us, let him say the Lord's Prayer for us poor sinners. So the second is learned? Fine, let him teach us, let him write learned books. And the third is prudent? Well, let him govern us and become pope.'

Dear Abbot, why not carry on as you used to and write some letters of useful advice to me, a poor bishop, and to other Christians who have all kinds of difficulties in serving the public? Let a monk's voice from the depths of the Middle Ages shake us in our complex, dynamic modern life. You may do some good. Try it, anyway, Father Abbot, please. Yours, Albino Luciani.

To the Patriarch of Venice,

I accept, and start off by turning my own sentence upside down.

If he is prudent, let him rule, I wrote in those distant days. If he rules, let him be prudent, I write now. That is, have some good basic principles firmly fixed in your head and know how to adapt them to the circumstances of life.

What principles? Let me take a few haphazardly. An apparent, even a resounding success is really a failure if it is achieved by trampling on truth, justice and charity. The man at the top is at the service of the man beneath him: this applies to both master and servants. The greater the responsibility, the greater the need for help from God. Your Metastasio says it himself: 'It needs both art and good sense to undertake anything good, but art and sense are no use without God.'

But high principles should be part of a man's life, and men are like leaves on a tree: all similar, none perfectly alike. They differ from one another according to culture, temperament, heredity, circumstances, and state of mind.

Let us look, then, at the circumstances and state of mind: if they change, you must change not the principles but their application to the reality of the moment. Christ once fled from the crowd that had come to carry him away and make him King. But when the circumstances changed, on the eve of the Passion, he himself prepared for the modest triumph of his entry into Jerusalem.

Excessive ease in changing is not what I call prudent, though. Good tactics in making changes at the right rate and adapting to them are not the same thing as opportunism and flattery, ignoring the man who has failed, playing fast and loose with one's own soul and principles. When a minister or a politician falls, how often does a great empty space open up around him. How often do we see turncoats!

Let me give an example. It is far away in time but a classic case . . . In 1815 the official French newspaper, *Le Moniteur*, showed its readers how to follow Napoleon's progress: 'The *brigand* flees from the island of Elba'; 'The *usurper* arrives at Grenoble'; '*Napoleon* enters Lyons'; 'The *Emperor* reaches Paris this evening.' What an amazing turnabout! This must not be compared with prudence, just as it isn't prudent to have a stubborn attitude and take no account of what is obviously real or to become excessively rigid and zealously upright, more royalist than the king, more papist than the pope.

This happens. Some people seize on an idea, then bury it and guard it for the rest of their lives, defending it jealously without ever examining it again, without ever trying to check what has become of it after all the rain and wind and storms of events and changes.

Those who travel in the stratosphere are in danger of not being prudent, when they are full of knowledge acquired purely from books. They can never get away from what is written, are always busy analysing, pointing out subleties, perpetually splitting hairs.

Life is quite another matter. Lord Palmerston rightly remarked that in cutting the pages of a book, a bone paper-cutter is much better than a sharp razor. Clemenceau, the tiger, felt the same when he passed judgement on two ministers in his cabinet: 'Poincaré knows everything but understands nothing,' he said. 'Briand knows nothing but understands everything.'

I would say: try to know and to understand at the same time. As I said before, have principles, then apply them to reality. That is the beginning of prudence. Yours, Bernard of Clairvaux.

To the Abbot of Clairvaux,

Thank you for your letter. I appreciate above all your encouragement to us to re-examine things, to check the truth of things, not to let situations stagnate, and to put in hand the necessary reforms. This is right for the Church, for the state, and for any town council.

'Do you know what's happened?' a mayor said to me. When a man was appointed to the council, he noticed that a public employee was sent to stand by some seats in the public gardens every day. What a waste, he thought. It could be explained if he were guarding the Bank of Italy, but what was he doing beside ten modest seats? The man decided to look into it and this is what he found: years earlier the garden seats had been repainted. To prevent anyone spoiling the wet paint, a guard had been placed there on orders from the council. They forgot to rescind the order, the paint dried, and the guard remained, guarding nothing.

To go back to the prudence of rulers: Father Abbot, don't you think there has to be something dynamic about it? Plato called prudence the coachman of virtue; well, the coachman is trying to get to his destination, sparing his horse's life if he can; but if need be he uses the whip and even hurts the horse in order to arrive on time. In other words, I don't want to confuse prudence with inertia, laziness, somnolence or passivity. It excludes blind zeal and mad ardour, but it wants bold, frank, decisive action when need be. Sometimes it uses the brake, sometimes the accelerator; sometimes it urges us to spare ourselves, sometimes to go flat out; sometimes it restrains our

54

speech, our hopes, our anger; sometimes, when there's good reason for it, it allows them to burst out.

In the years when Cavour's emissaries were working for the Romagna, Paolo Ferrari the playwright came to Turin and said to him: 'Count, we don't know whom to believe: Buoncompagni advises prudence and La Farina boldness. Which of them interprets your way of thinking, who is the man you have really sent?' 'Both,' replied Cavour. 'You need bold prudence and prudent boldness.'

I await your comments. Yours, Albino Luciani.

To the Patriarch of Venice,

Bearing in mind the fact that Cavour may not have been quite serious in his answer, I agree that prudence should be dynamic and urge people to action. But there are three stages to consider: deliberation, decision, and execution.

Deliberation means seeking the means that lead to the end. It is made on the basis of reflection, of advice that has been asked for, of careful examination. Pius XI often used to say: 'Let me think first.' The Bible warns us: 'Son, do nothing without advice.' Popular proverbs confirm this: 'Four eyes see better than two', 'Act in haste, repent at leisure', 'The fast runner seldom wins the race', 'The hasty cat had blind kittens'.

Decision means, after examining the various possible methods, make up your mind to use one of them: 'I choose this one, it's the most suitable and the only one that can be carried out.' Prudence isn't an everlasting see-saw, suspending everything and tearing the mind apart with uncertainty; nor is it waiting in order to decide for the best. It is said that politics is the art of the possible, and in a way this is right.

Execution is the most important of the three: prudence, linked with strength, prevents discouragement in the face of difficulties and impediments. This is the time when a man is shown to be a leader and guide. Philip of Macedon was referring to this time when he said: 'Better an army of timid

55

deer led by a lion than an army of strong lions led by a deer!'

Being a monk, I have to call prudence a virtue; and so it serves only noble causes and uses legitimate methods.

According to Plutarch, Alcibiades was obsessed by the need for popularity; he wanted to be noticed, at any price. When the public interest in his affairs waned what did he do? He had a very beautiful dog, for which he had paid an enormous sum, and he cut off its tail. This meant that the whole of Athens had reason to talk of Alcibiades, of his richness and his expensive oddities.

This wasn't prudence, but cunning, which I see works in your world through other methods: photographs published in the newspapers, press releases, carefully prepared speeches, artfully propagated rumours. Add to this the astute use of dishonest methods, and I can see you all belong to the school of the fox, of Ulysses and Machiavelli.

When the astute man speaks, his words are not a vehicle of his thoughts, but a veil over them, making the true appear false and the false true. Sometimes he achieves results. But as a rule these are not lasting. Furriers use more foxes' skins than they use those of asses. When the cunning walk in procession, it's the devil who carries the cross in front!

Forgive my frankness. Bernard of Clairvaux.

To the Abbot of Clairvaux,

According to your last letter, there are false kinds of prudence, such as dishonest cunning and astuteness, which you described. Sometimes, though, you can't deny that public men's lives would be difficult without recourse to cunning now and then. Think only of political candidates, who have to persuade the electors to elect them out of dozens standing for office, or of those already elected, who have to cultivate their electoral garden while thinking of re-election when the time comes.

In your own country of France, a short while ago, a small book appeared called *Piccione vola*. First of all it deals with what it calls blah-blah-blah, in other words the art of talking on and on until something worth saying has been found. Secondly, it explains the technique of presenting statistics, percentages and numbers, which are expecially useful in interpreting election results. When dealing with numbers it says: 'Democracy isn't ruled only by the law of numbers but by the law of *figures*.' Thirdly, it examines fine phrases which mean nothing at all.

Another book came out at the same time which was intended to help people avoid trouble in this kind of world; a compendium of speeches and sayings for people in politics. Think of that! There were thirty-two properly prepared and quite disparate ways of commemorating the dead, eighteen ways of handling condolences to their families, eighteen for starting a toast and fourteen for finishing one! A number of rules were suggested for toasts: they must be made holding the glass, and the length of the speech must vary in accordance with the speaker's inspiration, the importance of the person honoured, and the quality of the drink. There are also rules for funeral speeches: don't praise too much, but praise enough, praise politely, don't be snide in your praises.

In other words, it's a manual of small, almost harmless craftiness, rather like the 'witty inventions' of Goldoni's Lelio. We must allow them, don't you agree? Yours, Albino Luciani.

To the Patriarch of Venice,

I think you must be joking in your last line. I am all for correctness and consistency in public men, if for no other reason than that their behaviour determines the politeness or the rudeness of the young. On the other hand, they can help themselves by legitimate methods that are much more effective than those you mention. Wisdom, for instance. The wise man does not allow himself to be dazzled by appearances and by praise: he sees the temperament and ambitions of others in their faces and gestures. They may urge him to intervene at once but he may feel the time is not yet ripe; they may tell him it is best to wait, and he, with a sixth sense, may realize it is time to hurry; the facts may later prove him right.

It is also helpful to be methodical. This means putting the end before the means, linking the means to one another and giving each the weight it deserves. The rules this suggests are better than those of *Piccione vola* which you mention.

1) In deliberating, take account only of facts that have been checked. I say *facts*, not opinions or rumours; I say facts 'that have been checked' and not merely facts 'that are certain', because if I am a public administrator proofs need to be valid not merely for me but for everyone; they must be capable of being examined later on and standing up to criticism. The English describe something as being 'as safe as the Bank of England': this means it is the only thing which is entirely, indisputably true.

2) Remember an emphatic closing sentence which we used a great deal in the Middle Ages: *Distingue frequenter*. At the court of Louis XIV a lady could greet ten people with a single bow; there was only one bow, but her expression sent out all kinds of subtle flashes to give each one—duke or marquis or count or whatever he was—what was his due. By distinguishing we say: this business is important, I'll give it absolute precedence; this is less important, I'll give it second place. The famous 'choice of priorities'!

3) The Romans' expression 'divide and rule' is another you may

find useful. But I mean dividing actions into periods of time and not people from one another. For what reason? You can't do more than one thing well at a time!

Division, then, should apply to work as well as to other things; we must divide it by distributing it among a number of collaborators. But then we must use these collaborators! It mustn't be as it was in the days of the Triple Alliance, when people said: The Triple Alliance is the Double Alliance, that is, Bismarck. I think that with all the democracy you go in for, Bismarcks aren't too popular among you!

Would you like some more advice? *Foresight.* In 1800, Napoleon, before leaving Paris for Italy, stuck a pin into the map at a point between Alexandria and Tortona and said: 'Here, very likely, the Austrians will be concentrated.' He was a prophet; that was exactly where they concentrated, at Marengo.

Not everyone can have so prophetic a finger as that; but we should all try to make out the effects of our actions in the distant future and to calculate ahead how much effort and money will be needed for a particular initiative. Your minister Sonnino used silence as a means of being prudent. A friend once met him looking serious and thoughtful and said to him: 'I bet you're thinking of what you're going to say tomorrow in the Chamber'. 'Oh no,' replied Sonnino, 'I'm thinking of what I mustn't say.' Luzzati said of him: 'At Versailles, Orlando speaks in all the languages he doesn't know, and Sonnino keeps quiet in all the languages he does know.'

It may happen, though, that in spite of all that has been done, the undertaking goes wrong. The man in public life prepares himself for this possibility with adequate measures. The peasant thinks hail may come down on him and takes precautions. The general arranges everything with victory in mind; but he does keep something in hand, in case the defeat or retreat he prays won't happen in fact takes place.

Plutarch tells us that one day Diogenes began asking a marble statue for alms. Of course he didn't get a single coin, but he carried on asking. 'Aren't you wasting your time?' someone asked him. 'It's not a waste of time,' he replied, 'I'm getting used to being refused.' That was prudence, as well!

One final piece of advice. Don't be discouraged too much. Don't say: 'I've been sweating away for years working for the community. I've put everything into it, even neglecting my own interests and my family, and shortening my life with serious, persistent worries. And what happens? People avoid me, cut the ground under my feet, attack me, knock me down. Well, let them get on with it, I'm going to retire in good order!' The temptation is strong, but it's not always prudent to give way to it. Admittedly it's necessary to use people in rotation, but it's also true that the public good sometimes needs the man who's started to carry on, and the man who has talent and experience to stay. We should all take note of fair criticism (no-one's infallible!), but we must also remember that even Christ wasn't able to please everyone. When we work for the public, we mustn't long for too much approval and applause, but prepare ourselves for indifference and criticism from those we've been administering, whose psychology can be very odd.

Aristide Briand, who was prime minister of France several times, described it. A madman came into a shop, he said, carrying a hammer; he swung it at the china and smashed it all to pieces. People stopped, rushed across from elsewhere, and gazed in astonishment. Some hours later a little old man came into the shop with a box under his arm: he took off his coat, put on his glasses and very, very patiently, among all those broken pieces, began mending the pots. No one, you can be perfectly sure, stopped to watch *him*! Yours, Bernard of Clairvaux.

JOHANN WOLFGANG VON GOETHE, German poet (1749–1832), one of the greatest geniuses of Western literature. He was one of the leaders of the German literary movement known as *Sturm und Drang*, and through such works as *Die Leiden des Jungen Werthers* and his masterpiece *Faust*, he exercised a dominant influence on the development of German literature.

To Johann Wolfgang von Goethe

Illustrious poet,

The last Venice Film Festival (1971), which was talked about so much and in so many ways, made me think of you— I don't know why. Perhaps because of ideas called up from my subconscious by articles read in the papers at the time, mentioning you as an aesthete, an artist and an art critic.

You were a great aesthete because you were capable of perceiving, both intensely and widely, the beauty of the world, from natural phenomena to the powerful passions of the human spirit. You were a great artist because you were capable of expressing powerfully for others both the beauty you perceived and the states of mind with which you perceived it. You were an outstanding art critic because you looked with understanding and passion at the artistic creations of others.

Didn't Germany admire you for twenty-five years as the director of the theatre in Weimar? Didn't you call the day on which you set foot in Rome, the Rome of the ancient monuments, your second birthday? Didn't you almost faint with happiness in contemplating the Belvedere Apollo? What a pity you couldn't have contemplated the films in the Festival and that I couldn't have watched your reactions. So I'll try and guess them!

* * *

As an aesthete, you would have found many fine things that were new to you in the Festival. The film, composed, as it is, of light, movement, colours, music and action, is a beautiful thing.

You sit before a screen. If the direction of the film has been successful, you will be taken through what happens at a very fast rhythm, and time will fly past. Close-ups, which fill the screen with a single face, bring the figures extraordinarily close to you, showing people overwhelmed with deep feeling and creating a sense of great intimacy between you and the actors. The powerful foreshortening you admired in Mantegna and Caravaggio can be seen on a very large scale in the cinema, owing to the way in which—let's say—a villain is shown from below, his appearance altered by sinister shadows that make him look threatening and terrifying. This is just one cinematic effect among many.

Would you also find artistic beauty in the cinema? I think so. But the art critic in you would have to prepare for a surprise. You were used to contemplating things transcendentally, to fervent classicism, and to hearing a language that you had learnt from architecture, from marble statues and frescoes, from miniatures in codexes. You judged architecture, painting and acting individually.

In the cinema, though, there may be many artists involved: the director, the script writer, the actor, each working in understanding and in harmony with the others to produce a single film. But it is hard to decide which was the true creative moment: that varies from film to film. There may be art in it— I repeat—and art at a very high level; but if there is, it is not found in this or that part of the film, it wanders and scurries about in every part of it. It is an art *sui generis*; they call it the 'Tenth Muse'.

As for its influence, after parliament, the cabinet, the legal system and the press, it has become the fifth power. As for its range, it can now be called the first power. Some films have influenced millions of spectators across the years. Certainly it can condition people. But it is itself conditioned because it is linked to industry, and therefore to money. The director and the actors often wish to produce work at a high level artistically, work which allows them to reveal themselves.

But the producer, who must put down the money, argues otherwise and wants films that are successful. If a wizard existed —your Faust, let's say, or even Mephistopheles himself—who, by waving a magic wand or producing a magic potion, could guarantee in advance the success of an artistically good film, then the producer would make a film that was artistically good.

Not being wizards, producers resort to other expedients. Such as? Terence in his day was bitterly surprised to see the audience leaving his plays in order to go and laugh their heads off at clowns and mimes who had come to put on shows near the theatre.

This kind of thing keeps happening still: the producers tend to produce films that comply with the audience's least noble tendencies, an audience that goes to the cinema as a rule not to be elevated but to be entertained.

Here, then, is something at the Festival that would probably have saddened you as an art critic: realizing that there were the means and the people to make masterpieces, and instead sometimes finding works made with mediocre ingredients, because of the present preoccupation with money.

* * *

You might have noted another thing: films in which authentic artistry was mixed with equally authentic immorality. You may be surprised to find me admitting the existence of works that are immoral and at the same time artistically beautiful.

I use the word 'artistry' and 'artistically beautiful' in referring to the film itself; whereas I use the word 'immoral' in referring to the behaviour of the artist as a man and as a Christian. Certain immoral stories of Boccaccio are artistically fine; but in writing them Boccaccio committed a morally bad action that causes harm to some readers.

You know something about this yourself, for after you had written *The Sorrows of Werther* you felt uneasy and disturbed, noting its corrosive effect on the weakest and most excitable German youngsters.

* * *

But here I am, daring to put forward criticisms to you, who wrote of one of your own critics: 'Every artist, like every rose, has his insects; I have Tieck!' Well, now you have me too. I admire your genius, but don't accept some of your ideas. This, for instance: that as the whole of reality is the field of art, the artist may rightly and very freely narrate, paint, and describe everything, even evil.

Yes, the artist may represent evil, but only in a way that makes the evil appear evil, something to be avoided. It must not be believed, it must not be made beautiful, it must not encourage others to repeat and imitate it.

In the *Oedipus Rex* of Sophocles, the central theme is incest. This is described in crudely powerful language, but disapproval is so obvious from beginning to end, the punishments that fall on

the guilty are so terrible, that the reader is left pretty un-
enthusiastic about incest when he has finished reading.

I have written 'from beginning to end'. I say this with good
reason because there are directors and critics who think they can
redeem the whole of a pornographic film with a single sequence
or a moralistic touch at the end, brought in like a sprinkling of
holy water in an exorcism or some magic to ward off the evil eye.

It needs more than that!

* * *

There is another idea that must be rejected: that the man of
genius is a demigod—a star!—someone above ordinary morals.
You yourself expressed this thought, especially at the time in
which you were studying Spinoza with Madame von Stein, and
were seeking God in the 'Great Whole'. You believed then that
the intelligent man could, by rising higher and higher through
culture, be gradually absorbed by God, melting into Him and
becoming a law unto himself.

Today, many people share this idea, at least in practice. This
is wrong. Man's destiny and possibilities are certainly great, but
this greatness includes everyone, even the poorest, the most
ignorant and unfortunate. God wishes us all to be his children
and to have, in a way, his own destiny. But we must be elevated
through his help and by observing the laws which apply to us all,
great and small, including artists.

You, great poet, the artists whose works are shown at the
Festival, and we, the men in the street, less gifted with natural
talent, are all in this way equal before God. If someone is gifted
with artistic talent, and achieves fame and riches, this means he
has a greater obligation than others to show his gratitude to God
by leading a good life.

Being one of the great ones of the world is also a gift of God,
which should not make us proud but should urge us, instead,
towards modesty and virtue.

Once again, *noblesse oblige*!

DAVID, king of Judah and Israel (1013?–973 BC). One of the greatest Hebrew national heroes, celebrated not only as a warrior and ruler, but also for his gifts as a poet and musician. He was reputed to be the author of many of the Psalms, and according to the Gospels, Jesus was of the House of David.

To King David

Illustrious sovereign, poet and musician,
People see you in so many different ways.

Artists have depicted you for centuries—sometimes with a lyre, sometimes facing Goliath with a sling, sometimes on the throne, holding a sceptre, sometimes in the cave of En-gedi, cutting the skirt of Saul's robe.

Children love your fight with Goliath and your exploits as a bold, generous leader of a band of fighters.

The liturgy records you above all as an ancestor of Christ.

The Bible shows the various components of your personality: poet and musician; brilliant officer; successful king, involved—alas, not always happily—with intrigues over women and the family tragedies that come out of them; and in spite of that a friend of God, thanks to a remarkable piety that made you always aware of your smallness in relation to God.

This awareness is something I like particularly in you, and it makes me happy when I meet it, in, for instance, the short Psalm 131 which you wrote.

*   *   *

In this psalm you say 'Lord, my heart is not haughty'. I try to follow you, but have to confine myself to praying: 'I wish my heart not to chase after thoughts of pride! . . .'

That's too little for a bishop, you may say. I know, but the truth is that I've buried my pride a hundred times, deluding myself that I've buried it deep in the ground; and yet I've seen it come back a hundred times, livelier than ever: criticism still upsets me, praise delights me, and I worry over other peoples' opinion of me.

When I am given a compliment, I must compare myself with the donkey that carried Christ on Palm Sunday. I must say to myself: 'Suppose the donkey had grown proud when he heard the applause of the crowd, and, being the donkey he was, had bowed right and left to thank it, like a prima donna. How people would have laughed! Don't look as silly as that!' This is what I must tell myself.

When I am criticized I must put myself in the situation of Manzoni's Fra Cristofero, who, when people laughed and sneered at him, kept calm and said to himself: 'Brother, remember you're not here on your own account.' On another occasion, though, this same Fra Cristofero is seen 'receding a couple of paces, leaning proudly on his right foot, putting his right hand to his hip, pointing the other with outstretched forefinger towards Don Rodrigo, and fixing on him a pair of blazing eyes'. Christians today love that gesture: they like prophecies, noisy denunciations, flaming eyes, Napoleon-style flashes and fulminations.

I prefer what you write, King David: 'My heart is not haughty, nor mine eyes lofty.' I should like to approach the way of Francis de Sales, who wrote: 'If someone, in hatred, were to pluck out my left eye, I think I could still look kindly at him with my right one. If he plucked that one out too, I would still have my heart with which to love him.'

*   *   *

In your psalm you continue: 'Neither do I exercise myself in great matters, or in things too high for me.' This is a noble state of mind, if you compare it with what Don Abbondio* says: 'Men are made in such a way that they always want to go up, always up.' I fear, alas, that Don Abbondio was right: we try to reach those who are above us; to push our equals beneath us; and to make those already beneath us even further away.

We try to come out on top, to become important in order to have recognition, advancement and promotion. There's nothing wrong in that so long as it is a matter of healthy emulation, and moderate, reasonable desires that stimulate us to work and study.

But suppose it becomes a kind of illness? Suppose we trample on others unfairly, and run them down, in order to get ahead?

---

* A character in Manzoni's *The Betrothed*.

Suppose, to get further ahead, we 'gang up', under the most specious excuses, but really to stop other people, with even greater ambitions, from getting ahead?

And what satisfaction does that bring? Things at a distance, before we reach them, look different from the way they do when we come close to them.

In Psalm 52 you wrote against evil tongues, which, you said, were like 'a sharp razor'; instead of cutting the beard it cut peoples' good name. That's true. But once the razor has gone over it, the beard grows thickly again. Honour and fame that have been tarnished will grow bright again too. For this reason it's sometimes wise to be silent, to have patience: everything gradually goes back into place of its own accord!

*   *   *

In spite of everything we must be optimistic. This is what you meant when you wrote 'as a child that it weaned of his mother: my soul is even as a weaned child'. Faith in God must be the pivot of our thoughts and actions. Come to think of it, there are two main characters in our lives: God and ourselves.

When we look at the two, we shall always see goodness in God and know that wretchedness in ourselves. We shall see that God's goodness is well disposed towards our wretchedness and know that our wretchedness as the object of divine goodness. The opinion of others hardly matters: it doesn't cure a guilty conscience or hurt an upright one.

At the end of the short psalm your optimism bursts out in a joyous cry: 'Let Israel hope in the Lord from henceforth and for ever.' When I read you, you seem in no way afraid; a strong courageous man who emptied his soul of trust in himself in order to fill it with the trust and strength of God. In other words, humility goes with magnanimity. To be good is a great, fine thing, but it is difficult and arduous. To prevent the soul aspiring to great things in an exaggerated way, we need humility; and in order to avoid being afraid in the face of difficulties, we need magnanimity.

I am thinking of St Paul: contempt, whippings, pressures of

all kinds did not depress this magnanimous man; ecstasies, revelations, and applause did not exalt this humble man. He was humble when he wrote that he was 'less than the least of all saints'. He was magnanimous and open to any peril when he said: 'I can do anything in him who gives me strength.' Yes, he was humble, but at the right time and in the right place he could be proud: 'Are they Hebrews? so am I . . . Are they ministers of Christ (I speak as a fool) I am more.' He set himself below everyone else but when need be he refused to bow to anything or anyone.

The waves flung the ship that carried him onto the rocks; vipers bit him; pagans, Jews and false Christians pursued and persecuted him; he was beaten with rods and put in prison, he was made to die every day. People thought they had frightened and finished him, but he leapt out, fresh and radiant, to reassure us: '*Non angustiamur*,' he said, 'I do not despair.' Then he rose to his feet and flung out his defiant Christian certainties: 'Neither death, nor life, nor angels, nor principalities, nor powers, nor things present, nor things to come, nor height, nor depth, nor any other creature, shall be able to separate us from the love of God, which is in Christ Jesus our Lord.'

This is the outlet of Christian humility. It comes not from timidity but from courage, from enterprising work and surrender to God.

PENELOPE, wife of Ulysses, mother of Telemachus. She kept her suitors at bay during her husband's absence by promising to make her choice after finishing a piece of cloth, which she wove during the day and undid at night. She is a symbol of the woman who is faithful in good times and bad.

To Penelope

Princess,

Television has brought the story of Dido to our notice again. She ruled in Carthage in the years in which you were married to Ulysses, King of rocky Ithaca. What happened to her was sad and human.

St Augustine, who was bishop very near to Carthage, wept over her story when he was a boy, and we too were unable to hear it again without being moved.

Poor Dido, she swore to be faithful to her husband Sichaeus, and tried to control her growing passion for Aeneas; then trustfully, she gave herself up to love.

Then came tragedy; Dido guessed that Aeneas was preparing to leave Carthage. In vain did she beg her beloved hero to stay; in vain did she accuse him of ingratitude and betrayal. Aeneas left, and Dido, abandoned, could not bear her sorrow. The flames of the pyre she lit were seen by the Trojan ships on their way to Italy.

You, princess, were more fortunate and provided a better example. The wise Ulysses, with his protean mind, took you to his kingdom after setting the marriage-bed solidly under the most thriving olive-tree. By him you had a wonderful son, Telemachus.

Admittedly Ulysses left almost at once for the long Trojan war, and when it was over (thanks, in particular, to the famous wooden horse he built) he was forced to sail over the seas of half the world.

But in spite of his many vicissitudes, he was lucky enough to return to his Ithaca and to your love, which in the meantime you had kept sweet-scented and untouched. Those tiresome suitors, who had settled in your house and were banqueting merrily at your expense, urged you to choose a new husband among them. But you refused. While they were banqueting downstairs you and your handmaidens upstairs wove fabric during the day and undid the work at night, in order to keep them at bay and defend your fidelity in love.

Every night your heart and your dreams told you that your husband would return. Who, then, could ever be so bold as to try to sleep on Ulysses's pillow, drink from his cup, give orders to his now adult son, ride his horse, and call his dog?

The suitors were all shot with arrows, fidelity had its reward, the family was reunited, and conjugal love restored.

*　*　*

This love, which was sacred to you, Princess, is still sacred to us Catholics. And it should not be joked about.

Montaigne, for instance, depicts marriage as a kind of painted, gilded cage: the birds outside it are trying frantically to get in, and those inside it doing all they can to get out.

The Second Vatican Council, on the other hand, notes with pleasure that 'many men of our age value highly the true love between husband and wife'.

Among the biblical passages it quotes is the following, which might have been written for the return of your husband: 'Rejoice with the wife of thy youth. Let her be as the loving kind and pleasant roe.' (Proverbs, 5,18–19). Think no more of the witch Circe, Ulysses, who kept you in her palace, feasting and carousing for a whole year; think no more of the beauty of Nausicaa, the girl you saw fleetingly at the river bank. If your journey is to take place again, have yourself tied once more in the hold of the ship, to avoid being lured by the sirens' song.

There is a passage in the Council's findings that suits you very well, Princess. It speaks of conjugal love which is 'indissolubly faithful in good times and bad, on the level of the body and of the spirit, and alien to adultery and divorce'. You achieved this love by practising 'uncommon virtue' and the

'... marriage ... a kind of painted, gilded cage ...'

'greatness of soul and spirit of sacrifice' mentioned by the Council, thus overcoming the many obstacles placed in the way of conjugal love.

The first of these is our *poor heart*, which is so changeable and unpredictable. The wise spouse knows that it must be kept under control. He may delude himself that he can sometimes cease to keep guard and allow himself some 'distraction'. 'It's only for a moment,' he tells himself. 'I won't go outside the fence, I'll just glance over the top of the gate, which is shut, to see how life goes on outside.' But what may happen is that the gate may be open by chance, the moment may become an hour and the hour may become a betrayal.

'What do you think you are doing?' St Francis de Sales wrote. 'You want to arouse love, don't you? But anyone who consciously arouses it is of necessity caught by it; in this game, he who takes is taken...'

Someone may think: 'I'd like to try it, but not too much'. Alas, the fire of love is more active and overwhelming than it seems. You think you are touched by a mere spark and to your astonishment find that a flame has been lit in your heart, that your resolutions have been reduced to ashes and your reputation has gone up in smoke.

* * *

The second obstacle is *monotony*. Every day, married people have to deal with the prosaic necessities of home and work. The husband is afraid his friends will think him weak if he gives up the match to keep his wife company; the wife thinks she's wasting time if she stops doing the housework to chat with him for a while. And so they come to feel that more or less everything has been said in their affective life, that their love can be put into the past and its manifestations can become mere memories. This is a dangerous situation, often met when people are in their forties, a situation Paul Bourget analysed profoundly in his novel *Le Démon de midi*.

Venus or Adonis turns up in the person of an office colleague, male or female, who seems to provide more points of contact than the spouse.

Or else there's silly curiosity: 'I'd like to see if the appeal I once had still works.' Having found that it does, it's almost impossible not to let oneself be carried away.

Or else, with healthy convictions falling into disuse, people let themselves be carried along on the fashionable tide of the day: 'Everyone does it!' 'Betraying a wife or a husband? What a melodramatic way to put it! It's much simpler than that—a matter of seizing an opportunity, picking a rose.' 'Are married couples called to fidelity? Yes, but it may be a multiple fidelity. My finding another woman doesn't lessen my tenderness for the mother of my children, the one who brings them up, keeps house for me, does the shopping and cooking and so on.'

Are there any remedies against this kind of danger? Yes: the sense of our dependence on God; prayer, which obtains what our weakness lacks; and the art of renewing our love. The husband should always continue to court his wife a little; the wife should always seek to praise her husband, and be kind and attentive.

Francis de Sales writes: 'Love and fidelity, joined together, always generate intimacy and trust; for this reason, married saints exchange many caresses within their marriage.'

'Thus Isaac and Rebecca (the chastest married couple in ancient times) were seen through the window caressing each other in a way that, although there was nothing indecent about it, made Abimelech realize they could not be anything but husband and wife.'

'The great king, St Louis, was almost reproached for going too far in the small attentions needed for the preservation of conjugal love.'

* * *

The third obstacle is *jealousy*, which does not—as people sometimes think—ennoble love but humiliates and corrupts it. 'It is foolish to praise love by wishing to exalt it with jealousy. Admittedly jealousy is a sign of the greatness and strength of love, but not of its goodness, purity and perfection. In fact, the man who loves perfectly is sure that the beloved is virtuous and faithful; the man who is jealous doubts the fidelity of his beloved.' Thus says St Francis de Sales, who goes on: 'Jealousy in the end spoils the substance of love, because it produces disagreements and quarrels.'

These *disagreements* and *quarrels* are a fourth obstacle to married love; even the best couples have their moments of weariness and ill temper, for which they must find a remedy without breaking the peace. Is he in a black, frowning mood? That's the time for her to be full of sweetness. Is she nervous and tired? That's the time for him to keep calm, waiting for things to clear up. The important thing is for the two of them not to be on edge together; otherwise there will be a short circuit, a great flash, and words will escape that are sometimes only too true, and are the kind to arouse disappointment, rancour and hidden wounds.

Justice seems to demand that, if bad times really cannot be avoided, each partner should have a turn at being ill-tempered. Unfortunately, it sometimes happens that one has a monopoly of anger. In this case . . . all that can be done is for the other to be brave and have a monopoly of patience!

* * *

Princess, I realize that I have put together theory and practice, superimposing what you, who were not a Christian, did with an inate sense of honesty and delicacy on what the bishop Francis de Sales taught, enlightened by the Bible and sustained by great psychological acumen.

Might this be of some use to today's married people, who clearly find themselves in the midst of so many difficulties?

I hope so!

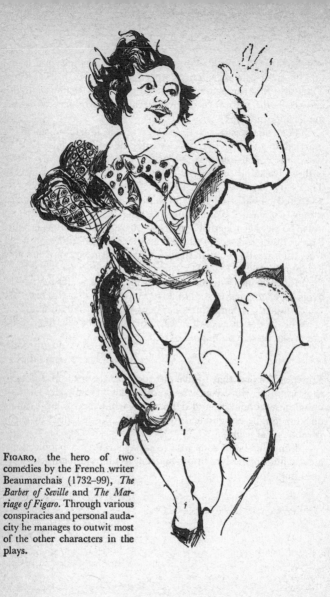

FIGARO, the hero of two comedies by the French writer Beaumarchais (1732–99), *The Barber of Seville* and *The Marriage of Figaro*. Through various conspiracies and personal audacity he manages to outwit most of the other characters in the plays.

To the Barber Figaro

Dear Figaro,

You're back! I've seen your *Marriage* on the television screen. You were one of the ordinary people of this world, yet you mixed with the privileged of your day as an equal. With your Susanna you represented youth struggling to have recognized its right to life, love, the family, and proper freedom. Compared with you and your air of enterprise and aggression, of youth and mischief, the nobility looked very pale and silly, a class on the point of collapse.

I've heard your famous monologue again. This is more or less what you say: 'What am I, if you compare me with all those noblemen who seem able to do everything, yet aren't really any better or any worse than me? I'm a barber, and a marriage-broker. Yes, but I'm something more—something new and strong. They want me to be the only honest man in a world of cheats and scoundrels. I won't accept that—I'm a *citizen*!'

That first evening in Paris, the theatre was in an uproar. The cheap seats applauded but the nobility was scandalized and stopped its ears. The king silenced you and put you in prison. In vain: from the stage and from prison you leapt into the market place, shouting: 'The play is over! The revolution is on the march!'

And you really opened up the French Revolution.

* * *

If you came back today, you would find that millions of youngsters are doing more or less what you did two centuries ago: they look at society and find it decrepit, they won't stand it and leap into the market places to hold forth.

In a Liverpool cellar there's a plaque saying 'The Beatles were born here! This is where it all began!'. You may not have heard of them, but they were four shock-headed young singers

81

with the same 'artistic air' as yours. The Queen of England not only did nothing to silence them—she gave them an important decoration.

They sold records by the million and made lots of money, and were applauded in theatres much larger than yours. As a result of their singing, groups arose all over the world, which sang to the accompaniment of drums and electric guitars, under powerful arc lights, twisting about and exciting their audiences to bouts of hysterical participation.

* * *

Look around you! Many of these youngsters wear a pigtail like you and give their hair an almost feminine amount of attention, using shampoos, having it waved and curled and even going to ladies' hairdressers for a 'set'. Not to mention beards! And whiskers and moustaches!

And what variety in clothes! A hotchpotch of old and new, masculine and feminine, East and West. A pair of blue jeans with a tee-shirt or a jersey or a leather jacket. Renaissance-style trousers, jackets like those of Napoleon's officers, trimmed with eighteenth-century-looking lace, and shoes with ecclesiastical buckles. Trousers and shirts in flaming colours and large floral patterns, with gypsyish overcoats. Clothes deliberately torn, suggesting some mythical country. And the girls wear mini skirts, shorts, maxi skirts, midi coats, all sorts of styles.

What d'you think of all this? I'm not really up to judging, but it all makes me feel curious, amused and a little critical. Their music is called 'young' music. But I can see that the sale of records rakes in millions for cunning old men.

They talk of spontaneity, non-conformity and originality; but in fact shrewd businessmen rule the clothes market undisturbed. Young men call themselves revolutionaries, but their rather too carefully done hair and exquisite clothes make them seem merely sissy. Girls wear very brief, smart, fashionable clothes. I don't want to be Manichan or Jansenist but I think, sadly, that it doesn't do much for the young men's virtue.

These youngsters all support 'the revolution', of course,

which they see as a way of making man cease to exploit his fellows.

Some of them think the present reforms are inadequate and counter-productive, and justify the revolution as the one and only means of achieving social justice.

Others want courageous social reforms that will come quickly. Only as a last resort, in very serious and exceptional circumstances, do they accept violence.

Others have lost all scruples. 'Violence is justified in itself and *the revolution must be made for it's own sake!*'

Mao Tse-tung told the Chinese: 'Let us set up the cultural revolution, clearing out the bourgeois ideology that has remained in Marxism.'

The Frenchman, Régis Debray, told the South Americans: 'Your revolution can't be the kind practised elsewhere, with a party to lead it. The true revolution is a guerrilla war involving the whole people.'

From Mao and Debray we go on to Fidel Castro, Giap and the French students of May 1968. 'The object of the students' revolution,' said Cohn-Bendit, 'is not to transform society, but to overthrow it.'

Clearly, dear Figaro, these all go further than you and follow your followers, Castro, Che Guevara, Ho Chi Minh and Giap. They all dream of becoming guerrilla fighters and desperadoes—with good intentions, of course. But they are used by others and don't realize that it is utopian to make a sharp and final division between the good and the bad, loyalty and oppression, 'progressives' and 'conservatives'. They don't realize that the disorder which arises within the 'spiral of violence' generally holds back progress by spreading discontent and hatred.

*   *   *

And yet, both of you can teach us a lesson, Figaro. This one, for instance: that all of us—parents, teachers, employers, priests and the authorities—have to admit that we certainly haven't been perfect in our dealings with the young, either in our methods or in our commitment, and that we must start all over again in a real spirit of humility and service, preparing ourselves to work slowly, carefully, undramatically.

A madman smashed a shop window with a stick and broke all the objects inside. In a moment the street was filled with people, gaping and discussing what had happened. Soon afterwards an old man arrived at the shop with a box under his arm. He took off his jacket, took glue, string and tools out of the box and with infinite patience began putting together the broken pieces. After hours and hours he finished. But no one stopped in the street or gazed curiously at what he was doing.

Something like this happens with the young. When they go in for rowdy demonstrations, everybody watches and discusses them. Meantime, slowly, carefully, patiently, parents and teachers are tidying things up, stopping up the holes, putting right their ideas; but no one sees them or applauds.

*　　*　　*

We must show ourselves more open and understanding towards the young and their mistakes. But we must call mistakes mistakes and present the Gospel unvarnished, and must not mess about with it because we love popularity. Some approval isn't right. 'Woe unto you, when all men shall speak well of you! for so did their fathers to the false prophets,' Christ said (Luke, 6, 26). Besides, the young love those who tell them the truth, and can see that real affection lies behind frank, loving warnings.

We must also accept that the young are different from ourselves in their way of assessing things, in their behaviour, in love and in prayer. They, like you, Figaro, have things to say that are worth listening to and worth respecting.

We must agree to share the task of forwarding society with them, on the understanding that they'll press harder on the accelerator and we'll press harder on the brake. In any case, the problems of the young can't be seen in isolation from the problems of society; their crisis is, in part, the crisis of society.

Figaro, you were very sharp in striking at abuses and weaknesses, but not so good at suggesting remedies. Your diagnosis of society was accurate, allowing for exaggerations, but you had no remedy to suggest.

And yet for today's youngsters, and for those of any age, there's a remedy. We must make them see that the right answer to the questions they ask are given not by Marcuse or Debray or Mao but by Christ.

Do they want fraternity? Christ said: 'You are all brothers.' Do they long for authenticity? Christ spoke out forcefully against hypocrisy. Are they against authoritarianism and despotism? Christ said that authority was service. Do they oppose formality? Christ opposed prayers recited mechanically, alms given only to look good, self-interested charity. Do they want religious freedom? Christ on the one hand wanted 'all men . . . to come to knowledge of the truth'; and on the other he imposed nothing by force and did not prevent contrary propaganda. He allowed the Apostles to abandon him, Peter to deny him, Thomas to doubt him. It's true that he asked, and still asks, to be accepted both as a man and as God, but not before we've looked into it and seen that he must be accepted; not without our free choice.

What do you say to that, Figaro? Your *protests*, and Christ's *proposals*, put together: won't they help both the young and society in general? I believe so, trustfully.

PICKWICK, SNODGRASS, TUPMAN AND WINKLE are the members of the Pickwick Club, the subject of the famous book *The Pickwick Papers* by Charles Dickens (1812–70). One of their exploits gives Cardinal Luciani an excuse for arguing against those who, whether or not in good faith, attack the Church through prejudice.

To the Members of the Pickwick Club

My dear sirs, I have always liked you so much!

You, Mr Pickwick, the chairman, who are as gentlemanly as Don Quixote, with the cheerful, loyal Sam Weller always at your heels, as full of wisdom and common sense as Sancho Panza; and you, Snodgrass, Tupman and Winkle, with your funny little ways: I like you all so much!

While I was reading about you your figures leapt like living people from the pages of Dickens, making me smile. Up to a point I understood how a dying reader could ask God to grant him a further ten days of life, which was the time he needed to get and read the last instalment of the book that immortalizes you.

But here you are, Mr Pickwick, on your knees before a chipped stone poking up out of the ground by a house door.

'This is very strange,' you say and wipe the dust off it with your pocket handkerchief. 'I can discern a cross, and a B, and then a T,' you say. 'This is important. This is some very old inscription.' You buy it for ten shillings from the owner of the house and carry it off to the inn with your friends.

The stone is laid on the table, and, then, we are told, 'the exultation and joy of the Pickwick members knew no bounds'. Later, you 'lectured upon the discovery at a General Club Meeting, convened on the night succeeding their return, and entered into a variety of ingenious and erudite speculations on the meaning of the inscription'.

With the learning that distinguishes you, Mr Pickwick, you wrote a pamphlet containing twenty-seven different readings of the inscription. Your work was deservedly rewarded: 'seventeen native and foreign societies' elected you an honorary member for making the discovery.

But then what happened? An envious opponent appears in the person of Mr Blotton. This man goes to the spot where you found the stone, interrogates the man who sold it to you, and tells the Club that 'the man presumed the stone to be ancient, but solemnly denies the antiquity of the inscription—inasmuch as he represented it to have been rudely carved by himself in an idle mood, and to display letters intended to bear neither more or less than the simple construction of "Bill Stumps, his mark" '.

The reaction of the Club is immediate: Blotton is expelled with ignominy and you are offered 'a pair of gold spectacles in token of their confidence and approbation. . . . The seventeen learned societies unanimously voted the presumptious Blotton as an ignorant meddler'.

Now, between ourselves, we can say that it wasn't really an archaeological find but an ordinary stone. You were the victim of a serious mistake, Mr Pickwick, and in good faith took in your three friends, the entire Club, and the seventeen learned societies.

Well, it does happen. And just because it happens, and in order to make it happen as little as possible, St Thomas, a Doctor of the Church, wrote a pamphlet about mistakes of this kind and called it *De Fallaciis*. Would you allow me to discuss a few points with you? Yes? Thank you!

*   *   *

Your mistake, Mr Pickwick, would be called by St Thomas a 'paralogism', which means a false argument, but one put forward in good faith.

There are some of them to be found today: for instance, I often hear paralogisms from people who, in good faith, are hitting out at the Church. On the one hand, I suffer because I love the truth: the Church is actually quite different from what they think it is. On the other, I cheer myself a little when I see that they are often not so much against the Church as against the idea they have of it.

As a rule, these mistakes made in good faith, or paralogisms, are a result of prejudices that are about at the time, diffused by cutting slogans that are put out for purposes of propaganda. Today, for instance, such phrases as 'Church of the poor', 'treasures of the Vatican', 'Church allied with the powerful', make many people hostile to the Church, who until very recently loved and esteemed her unreservedly.

If these people are asked what they mean by 'Church of the poor', they probably can't really say. If they are told that the famous 'treasures' have no commercial value, that an annual income—even a large one—is needed by the Holy See, which has to deal with thousands of problems and needs (as well as, and above all, the problems of the poor), these same people partly give way and agree.

But there it is: propaganda goes on, prejudices bite into people's ideas, and mistakes cannot be avoided. One day God will judge all men—after considering their heads—and, I hope, in spite of their involuntarily twisted notions, will save them.

* * *

Not everyone who argues forcefully is in good faith like you though, Mr Pickwick. Some people deliberately try to mislead others with what they say. In their case we are dealing not with paralogisms but with 'sophisms', and ugly human passions enter into it. Which ones?

The first, I'd say, is the spirit of contradiction. You say something; he feels he must deny it. You deny it, he feels he must affirm it. You talk to him; and while you're talking, all he thinks about is how he can contradict you, refute you, and affirm his own views.

On a narrow bridge between the banks of a stream, a mule had stopped and dug his hoofs in firmly. People tried pulling him by the halter, and beating his ribs with a stick, but there was no way of making him move. On both sides of the bridge people waited impatiently.

'Let me have a go!' cried a man who should certainly have belonged to the Pickwick Club. He went up to the mule, seized its tail, and gave it a tug. Thinking he was being asked to go back, the mule shot forward like an arrow, and left the bridge clear.

Dear Mr Pickwick, we're often very much like that! We do what we think others wouldn't want us to do, and don't do what others want us to do. And when we behave like that we're not calm and straightforward in the way we think or the way we speak.

* * *

Have you ever heard of Mohs, Mr Pickwick?

He was a scientist who died in 1839, just two years before the publication of the minutes of your club. He produced the Mohs Scale, which shows, in ten ascending steps, the hardness of minerals; from *talcum* and *plaster* it goes up, getting harder and harder, right up to *diamond*.

Well, Mr Pickwick, you should tell Mohs that some heads seem even harder than diamond. They never give in, they seize a mistaken idea in the face of all evidence against it. Give a nail to a stubborn man, says the proverb, and he'll knock it in with his head!

Others are over-critical, pernickety, jibbing at everything, nagging at everyone, never pleased with anything or anybody.

Others are dogmatic. Because they've read some article or travelled or had some experience, they think they can teach everyone their business and that their opinion goes for everything.

Obviously the stubborn, the hypercritical and the dogmatic are inclined to error. Whereas someone with a modest estimate of himself, someone willing to listen to others, tends to tell the truth.

These kindly attitudes were shown by Mochi, our Florentine ethnologist, who was a contemporary of yours, Mr Pickwick, and who had travelled a great deal. 'Paris?' he would say. 'Yes, I've been there. It's like Florence, only bigger. As soon as you've finished with Florence, start another Florence, and then another. Several Florences put together would make Paris. Massaua? Yes, I've seen it: it's like Florence only smaller, without monuments, without the Viale dei Colli and without the *Nuovo Giornale*.' Very modest, as you see, and rightly so, because the less proud a man is the more he's likely to be free of insincerity and error.

* * *

Apart from personal pride, there's group pride, and this causes error as well. Take the party, the class, or the country. People seize on this or that idea not because it's known to be true but because it's the idea of the group, the idea of the party. From this flow the errors of racialism, nationalism, parish pumpery, and imperialism, embraced by millions.

From this too flow the errors produced by opportunism. Out of laziness or self-interest, we run with the crowd, feathers borne on the wind, driftwood tossed on the current. You fell into this mistake yourself, Mr Pickwick, in the famous electoral meeting when candidates and electors of the 'Blues' and the 'Yellows' were contesting the little town of Eatanswill.

Having left your coach with your friends you found yourself surrounded by an enthusiastic group of Blues, who asked you at once to cheer for their candidate Slumkey.

' "Slumkey for ever!" roared the honest and independent.

"Slumkey for ever!" echoed Mr Pickwick, taking off his hat.

"No, Fizkin," roared the crowd.

"Certainly not," shouted Mr Pickwick.

"Hurrah!" And then there was another roaring, like that of a menagerie when the elephant has rung the bell for the cold meat.

"Who is Slumkey?" whispered Mr Tupman.

"I don't know," replied Mr Pickwick in the same tone. "Hush, don't ask any questions. It's always best on these occasions to do what the mob do."

"But suppose there are two mobs?" suggested Mr Snodgrass.

"Shout with the loudest," replied Mr Pickwick. Volumes could not have said more.'

Alas, Mr Pickwick, when you get to the point of shouting with those who shout loudest anything may happen. And the mistakes can't always be repaired. You know yourself: a madman may throw a valuable bracelet down a well, and twenty wise men may not be able to get it out again.

If only everyone believed this, and no one played the madman!

PINOCCHIO, the main character in the book of that name by the
Florentine writer Collodi (pseudonym of Carlo Lorenzini), 1826–90.
Pinocchio is a puppet come-to-life, whose adventures teach him (and
his young readers) to distinguish right from wrong.

To Pinocchio

Dear Pinocchio,

I was seven when I read your adventures for the first time. You can't possibly imagine how much I enjoyed them and how often I read them again. In you as a child I recognized something of myself, and in your surroundings I saw my own.

You used to race through woods and fields, onto the beach and into the streets. And with you ran the Vixen and the Cat, the dog Medoro, the boys of the Battle of the Books. It all felt like the way I ran, like my friends, like the streets and fields of my own village.

You used to go and watch carriages arriving in the main square, and so did I. You wriggled and made faces and put your head under the bedclothes before taking a glass of nasty medicine, and so did I. A slice of bread buttered on both sides, a sweet with a soft middle, a sugar lump and sometimes even an egg or a pear, even the skin of a pear, were wonderful treats for the greedy, hungry boy you were; and so they were for me.

I too was involved in fights on the way to and from school: with snowballs in winter and fists at every other season. I took a bit and gave a bit, trying to keep my end up and not cry when I got home, because if I'd complained they'd have certainly finished off what the others had started!

Now you're back, no longer speaking from the pages of a book, but appearing on television. But you're still the child you always were.

Whereas I've grown old. I now find myself on what you might call the other side of the fence. And I can no longer recognize myself in you, only in your advisers: Mastro Geppeto, the Talking Cricket, the Blackbird, the Parrot, the Glow-worm, the Crab, and the Marmot. They tried—alas, unsuccessfully, except in the case of the Tunny Fish—to advise you on the best way to live your life as a child.

Now, I'm going to try and give you some advice for your future as a boy and a young man. And don't you lash out at me with that hammer of yours, because I'm not prepared to end up like the poor Talking Cricket.

* * *

Have you noticed that I didn't list the Fairy among your advisers? You see, I don't like her behaviour. When you were chased by murderers, you knocked desperately on the door of her house; she looked out of the window, her face waxen white, refused to open the door and let you be hanged.

She freed you from the oak tree later, that's true, but then she played a dirty trick on you by letting four jet-black rabbits into your room when you were ill; and the four of them were carrying a small bier on their shoulders.

And that wasn't all. Having escaped the green fisherman's frying-pan by a miracle, you went home soaked. It was pitch dark and the rain was pouring down. The Fairy arranged things so that the door was shut, and after you'd been knocking on it desperately she sent you the Snail, who took nine hours to get down from the fourth floor bringing you—who were half dead with hunger—some bread made of chalk, a chicken made of cardboard, and four alabaster apricots painted to look real.

Well, no-one should treat a boy like that when he makes a mistake, especially if he's entering or has entered the age known as 'difficult'; that is, the years from thirteen to sixteen, which you will be coming up to, Pinocchio.

Just wait: it *will* be difficult both for you and for your teachers. You're no longer a child, so you'll despise the company, books and games of children; you're not yet a man, so you'll feel misunderstood and almost rejected by adults.

Physically, you'll be growing fast, which is tiring, and will suddenly feel you've got hugely long legs, ape-like arms and a voice that changes oddly and unexpectedly.

You'll feel a powerful urge to assert yourself. On the one hand you'll be in opposition to your surroundings, at home and at school; on the other you'll rush into the solidarity of a gang. On the one hand you'll demand independence from your family; on the other you'll long to be accepted by your peers and to rely on them.

How scared you'll be of being unlike the others! Where the gang goes, you want to go. Where the gang stops, you want to stop. The others' jokes and language and doings have all got to be yours. What they wear you wear. One month all the boys are in tee-shirts and blue jeans. Next month they're all in leather jackets, bright trousers and black shoes with white laces. In some things you're all against conformity. In others, without your even realizing it, you're one hundred per cent conformist.

And your moods keep changing, too. Today you're as quiet and biddable as you were at the age of ten; tomorrow as sour as a liverish old fellow in his seventies. Today you want to be an airline pilot, tomorrow an actor. Today you're bold and free thinking, tomorrow timid, almost worried. How patient and indulgent, how loving and understanding your master Geppeto will have to have with you!

And, what's more, you'll become introspective, that is, you'll start looking inside yourself and discovering new things: you'll find melancholy sprouting in you, and the need to day-dream; you'll find sentiment and sentimentality. It may be that while you're still at school you'll fall in love, not like a little boy but like the young David Copperfield, who said:

'I adore Miss Shepherd, she is a little girl in a spencer with a round face and curly flaxen hair. The Misses Nightingale's young ladies come to the cathedral too. I cannot look upon my book, for I must look upon Miss Shepherd. In a service I mentally insert Miss Shepherd's name. I put her in among the Royal family. At home in my own room I am sometimes moved to cry out "Oh, Miss Shepherd", in a transport of love. Why do I secretly give Miss Shepherd twelve Brazil nuts for a present, I wonder. They are not expressive of affection yet I feel that they are appropriate for Miss Shepherd. Soft seedy biscuits also I bestow upon Miss Shepherd, and oranges innumerable. Miss Shepherd being the one pervading theme and vision of my life, how do I ever come to break with her? I can't conceive and yet a coolness grows between her and myself. Whispers reach me of Miss Shepherd's having said she wished I wouldn't stare so and having avowed a preference for Master Jones, for Jones, a boy of no merit whatever. At last one day I meet the Misses Nightingale's establishment out walking. Miss Shepherd makes a face as she goes by, and laughs to her companion. All is over. The devotion of a life—it seems a life, it is all the same—is at an end: Miss Shepherd comes out of the morning service and the Royal family know her no more.'

It happened to David Copperfield, it happens to everyone. It will happen to you too, Pinocchio!

* * *

But how will your advisers help you? When it comes to growing up your new Talking Cricket should be old Vittorino da Feltre, a teacher who loved children in his own time and gave enormous importance to open-air sports in education.

Riding, swimming, jumping, fencing, the chase, fishing, running, archery, singing: he meant all these to create a calm atmosphere in his 'Joyous House' and to give a useful outlet to his young pupils' physical exuberance. He would have agreed with what Parini said later: 'What can a bold spirit not do, with strong limbs full of life?'

Your friend the Tunny Fish, who carried you on his back safe and sound to the bank as soon as you came out of the swordfish's belly, could help you—being peaceful and persuasive—in the next important crisis of self-assertion.

Today, youngsters dream not just of automobiles but of a whole parking-lot of auto-morals, auto-choice, auto-decision, auto-government, autonomy; a while ago some boys in Bolzano actually set up an auto-school, to teach themselves!

Quite right to reach auto-decisions, to make up your own mind, the wise Tunny Fish would say peaceably. But a little at a time, step by step. You can't move abruptly from the child's obedience to the adult's full autonomy. Nor, today, can you use

96

3

the tough methods that were once in order. Gradually, as you grow older, Pinocchio, the desire for autonomy will grow in you. Well, with the help of good teachers, let the proper awareness of your rights and duties, and the sense of responsibility to use the autonomy you want so much, grow as well.

Listen to the way in which, over a century ago, the Visconti-Venosta brothers were educated. One, Giovanni, was a literary man, the other, Emilio, a politician in our Risorgimento. 'One of my father's ways of educating us was to spend us much time with us as possible, and to demand complete confidence from us, often exchanging confidences of his own for it, and treating us as if we were a little older than we were. In this way he inspired feelings of responsibility and duty in us. We were treated like young men, which flattered us a good deal, and meant that we felt committed to keeping ourselves up on that level.'

Like nearly all youngsters between the ages of seventeen and twenty, on your way to autonomy, you may strike against a hard rock—the problem of faith. In fact you'll breathe in anti-religious objections as you breathe the air at school, in the factory, in the cinema, and everywhere else. If you think of your faith as a heap of corn, then a whole army of rats will attack it. If it's a garment, hundreds of hands will try and tear it off you. If it's a house, a pickaxe will try and demolish it, bit by bit. You must defend it: today, only the faith that is defended survives.

There is a persuasive reply to many of the objections you will hear. To others, an exhaustive reply hasn't yet been found. What should you do? Don't fling away your faith! Ten thousand difficulties, Newman said, do not make a doubt.

And remember two things.

First: you must respect every certainty, even if it isn't of an obvious, mathematical kind. The fact that Napoleon, Caesar or Charlemagne existed isn't certain in the way that $2+2=4$ is, but it's certain in human and historical terms. In this way it's certain that Christ existed, that the Apostles saw him dead and then risen from the dead.

Second: a sense of mystery is necessary to man. We don't know everything about anything, Pascal said. I know many things about myself but not everything. I don't know exactly what my life is, or my intelligence, or the state of my health, and so on. How can I expect to understand and know everything about God?

The most frequent objections you'll hear will concern the Church. You may be helped by a remark quoted by Pitigrilli. In London, at Speaker's Corner in Hyde Park, a preacher kept being interrupted by a dirty unkempt man. 'The Church has existed for two thousand years,' this man shouted at one point, 'and the world is still full of thieves, adulterers and murderers.' 'You're right,' replied the preacher. 'Water has existed for two million years, and look at the state of your neck!'

In other words, there have been bad popes, bad priests and bad Catholics. But what does that mean? That the Gospel has been applied? No, just the opposite. In those cases the Gospel hasn't been applied.

Dear Pinocchio, there are two famous sentences about the young. I recommend you the first by Lacordaire: 'Have an opinion and make it work for you.' The second is by Clemencau and I don't recommend it at all: 'He has no ideas but defends them warmly.'

*　　*　　*

May I go back to David Copperfield? The memory of Miss Shepherd is now several years behind him and he is seventeen and in love again; this time he adores Miss Larkins. If he can bow to her just once during the day he is happy. His only relief lies in wearing his best clothes and continually polishing his shoes. 'I picture Mr Larkins waiting on me next morning and saying, "My dear Copperfield, my daughter has told me all, youth is no objection, here is twenty thousand pounds. Be happy!" I picture my aunt relenting and blessing us.' Meantime, Miss Larkins marries a hop grower.

'I am terribly dejected for about a week or two. I take off my ring, I wear my worst clothes, I use no bears' grease, and I frequently lament over the late Miss Larkin's faded flower.'

Later he falls in love with Dora. 'Life without Dora's love was not a thing to have on any terms. I couldn't bear it and I wouldn't. I had loved her every minute, night and day, since I first saw her. I loved her at that minute to distraction. I should always love her every minute to distraction. Lovers had loved before and lovers would love again but no lover who ever loved would, could, or should ever love as I loved Dora.'

These are transparent quotations: through them we can see the problems of love and engagement, which you must prepare yourself for, Pinocchio. In considering such things today, some people propose a broadly permissive morality. Even if we admit that we've been a little too strict in some ways in the past, we shouldn't accept this permissiveness, and nor should the young. Their love should have a capital L, it should be as fair as a flower, as precious as a jewel—not as ordinary as a glass of water.

They must accept some sacrifices and keep away from people, places and entertainments that are occasions for evil. 'You don't trust me,' you'll say. Yes, I do, but it isn't lack of trust to remember that we're all exposed to temptation. It's because I love you that I want to remove unnecessary temptations from your path.

Look at car drivers; they have traffic police, traffic lights, yellow lines, one way streets, no-parking zones; all things that at first sight seem irritating and restrictive. These rules seem made in opposition to the motorist but in fact they are in his favour because they help him to drive more safely and more agreeably.

And if one day you have a girl-friend—a Miss Shepherd or a Miss Larkins or a Dora—then respect her. Protect her against yourself. You'll want her to keep herself pure for you, won't you? That's just as it should be, Pinocchio, but do the same for her, and take no notice of the friend who tells you of his prowess with girls, bragging about his exploits and thinking himself no end of a dog on account of them. The man who can control himself is the one to admire; he's the strong man who belongs to the real aristocracy of souls. So long as you're engaged, love should give you not so much sensual pleasure as a delicate joy of the spirit: it should be shown with affection, of course, but correctly and properly.

The same sort of advice is given to the girl, if she will stand a little 'preaching'. Dear Dora (or Miss Larkins, or Miss Shepherd or whoever it is), her mother says, let me just remind you of a biological law. In matters of sex the girl as a rule has more control over herself than the boy. The man may be stronger physically, but the woman is stronger spiritually. It would even seem that God decided to make the goodness of man depend on the goodness of woman. Soon the souls of your husband and children will depend on you a little; today, those of your friends and the boy in love with you do the same. In the meantime you must have enough sense for both of you, and be able to say no in some things, even when everything seems to ask you to say yes. If the boy's any good, he'll be grateful to you in his best moments and say to himself: 'My Dora was right, she's got a conscience and obeys it. She'll be faithful to me later.' Whereas the girl who's too easy to get isn't as re-assuring, and if she gives in too easily she runs the risk of planting dangerous ideas in the boy, which later on, when he is her husband, will turn into jealousy and suspicion.

Well, that's it, Pinocchio. But don't tell me it was out of place to talk about Dora. When you were a child you had the Fairy, first as a sister, then as a mother. When you're an adolescent and a young man, a Fairy beside you can only be a girl-friend and a wife. Unless you become a monk!.

But I can't see signs of a vocation in you!

PAOLO DIACONI, an eighth-century monk and historian from Friuli, educated at Pavia at the court of King Ratchis, then tutor to the daughter of Desiderio Adelpaga. After the fall of the Longobards, he was taken to France where he met Charlemagne, at whose court he stayed for a long time as a teacher. He wrote many poems and a *History of the Longobards* which has linked his name with the history of the Middle Ages.

To Paolo Diacono

Illustrious historian,

The National Eucharistic Conference which is to take place in Friuli (August 1972) has made me think of you. Though your family came from Lombardy, you were born in Friuli and wrote of your people with a son's affection.

The Longobards who came to Italy twelve centuries ago amounted to several hundred thousand. You described them advancing along the Via Postumia and thought they looked like an army of ants on the march. .

Suppose you were to come back now? Imagine yourself on a Saturday or Sunday in July or August, sitting at the Fadalto Pass, counting the foreign and Italian cars going down to Caorle, Jesolo and Venice, or up towards the Cadore. Or else on the Brenner Pass, or other Alpine passes that are even more congested by tourists.

Suppose I tell you that in the few days of the August holiday a million Milanese will leave Milan, a million Romans will leave Rome, and an interminable procession of cars will proceed in all directions at all hours on all the roads of Italy? I can imagine your astonishment. 'But where are all these people going?' you'll ask me.

They go to the sea, to the mountains, to see interesting buildings and natural curiosities; they go in search of fresh air, greenery, sand, sea and ozone, they go in order to escape.

And where will they stay? All over the place; in hotels, boarding houses, tent towns or tourist villages, holiday houses, motels, camping sites. Do you see that little object on four wheels, hooked on to the back of the car? That's a caravan, a small travelling house.

In your day you stopped your horse and tied him to a tree. In ours people stop the car and caravan where there's a clump of trees and a stream. There, they take out a gas cylinder with a stove and a portable fridge, prepare food, have supper sitting on the grass, and enjoy the rustle of leaves blown by the wind, the buzzing of bees and insects, the scent of grass and flowers, the colour of the sky; in other words they enjoy being in close contact with nature, which both stimulates and calms the mind. In the caravan, among a hundred other things, are folding beds with foam mattresses; at night, holidaymakers put them out and sleep on them, expecting to be woken by birdsong. They want to steep themselves in nature, at least for a short while; they want to forget their usual worries and the city of brick and concrete that has swallowed them up before and will swallow them up again for many long months.

I see you with your head in your hands. 'Why, this is noisier than the old invasions!' you say. 'People have turned into snails, taking their houses along with them. Sometimes the house is on wheels. Sometimes it's a piece of white canvas folded up behind the car seat, then unfolded, spread out and raised a little to make a kind of room. Sometimes it's a huge blue tent lit by electric light, with a radio and a television set, in a row with lots of other tents all filled with people of every race and tongue. It's another Babel! I won't say another thing!'

Lucky you! I'm a shepherd of souls, though, and can't give up writing. And I must deal at least briefly with some of the problems of conscience involved in all this moving about, wandering—whatever you like to call it—at weekends, on short holidays, public holidays, ordinary holidays; tourism, holiday-making. Please follow me out of the corner of your eye, while I address my readers.

* * *

A classic case of the tourist for us Italians is Petrarch, who was a mountaineer and travelled wherever he could go, both inside and outside Italy, in search of the places, friends and books he loved. This travelling was good for his curiosity and his thirst for knowledge, but rather less good for his finances. Indeed his steward, Monte, used to grumble at him and say: 'With all this wandering, you'll always have empty pockets.'.

Well, here's my first thought: don't people sometimes spend too much on travel, a really unjustified amount? I'm not speaking of the odd case here and there. The mania for holidays, which makes people spend more than they can afford, is with us today as it was in Goldoni's time, often at the expense of duties and domestic qualities like a sense of economy and an idea of where to draw the line, and what to save.

* * *

Another thought. People say they travel in order to learn, to stretch their minds, to be able to talk to others, to enlarge their knowledge of the beauties of art and nature in other countries. All this is fine so long as the holiday goes ahead calmly, with enough pauses and proper preparation and an eye for what is useful and essential. It may even bring moral improvements, if we feel our own smallness in so large and beautiful a world; it may make us more grateful and bring us closer to God, and make us feel more united with our fellow men.

But people pine for holidays for no good reason. Some go to Rome, say, and when they get home can talk of nothing but a particular wine or restaurant they found there.

Some people seem to know nothing about history. Fucini had a guide who took him to see Sorrento. 'Well, while I'm having a bite,' he said to the guide, 'tell me where Tasso's house is.' The guide went off and came back again: 'The gentleman you mentioned has never been here,' he said. Then there's the bragging tourist who loves to astonish his listeners with marvellous tales, as if he were a Marco Polo or a Cabot.

* * *

A holiday means rest and relaxation. But some people know how to rest and some don't. It's like dusting; some housewives think they're dusting when they're just transferring dust from one place to another.

The family who, in order to follow the fashion, arrives at a crowded resort in the middle of August when the hotels are crammed and has to put up with what it can find—sleeping on makeshift beds that may even be a billiard table or a deck-chair—doesn't rest in the least but is exchanging tiredness for more tiredness, boredom for more boredom.

A man may drive a hundred and fifty kilometres on a Sunday to Cortino or Jesolo, along a road clogged with cars. After Mass he goes for a walk, has lunch and a chat; he then goes home, driving in an endless queue with other cars, constantly trying or managing to overtake, scraping his mudguards, going round awkward bends. If he gets home safe and sound he thanks God and says he's had a great outing, unlike the usual ones. But he doesn't say he's rested.

Plenty of people get back from holidays tired and fed up, because they chose a place that was too smart or too noisy, or because there were too many trips and outings, or because they got in with people who involved them in tiring, over-stimulating entertainments, discussions and talks. I mentioned roads clogged with cars, bends in the road, overtaking. This is another moral problem. It's odd that no driver ever says in the confessional: 'Father, I've put my life and other people's lives in danger', no-one who says: 'I've been rash and too aggressive when I drove the car.' Yet plenty of people say—almost swear—to themselves the minute they see a car in the distance: 'I'll overtake it.' Whatever make of car it is, they've got to overtake it; they've got to go down in history as champion overtakers. Or else they drive when they've had a lot to drink or when they're too tired or depressed or have serious personal worries. This is playing with the fifth commandment. We never lay stress enough on the grave responsibility anyone has who's driving today's powerful cars on yesterday's poor, narrow, twisting, much-used roads.

The fifth commandment deals not only with damage to bodies but with damage done to souls by bad example. The holiday-maker and the tourist is watched admiringly, or at least

curiously, by the poorest and the youngest. The tourist generally reasons like this: 'As I'm outside my usual circle, I can have more moral freedom.' Whereas in fact he should reason in the opposite way: 'I'm watched more closely away from home, so I must behave even better than I would at home.'

Renato Fucini, as a tourist in Sorrento, found that tourists are very carefully watched. The guide I've already mentioned was boasting that he could always tell where visitors came from. 'You're from Piedmont, for instance,' he said. 'No, I'm Tuscan. Didn't you know?' said Fucini.

'Your Excellency, you've used no bad words. You haven't sworn in the name of God,' said the guide. 'How could I imagine you were Tuscan?'

Well, let's hope more tourists turn out to seem Piedmontese! And, to take things the other way round, I hope people going on summer holidays choose places so Christian in spirit, tradition and way of life that what the first saint from the USA, Elizabeth Seton, wrote of a small town in Tuscany, where she stayed for a short time, could be said of them too. 'I assure you that my becoming a Catholic [she'd been a Protestant before that] was the result of having gone to a Catholic country,' she said.

* *. *

The sixth commandment may also be put at risk on holiday. This involves ways of dressing, young people taking holidays together, unsuitable entertainments in many holiday places, and long car rides taken by two people alone, whether they're engaged or not.

As far as dress is concerned, people say: 'Oh, everyone dresses like that!' That's not true, not everyone does, though it must be admitted, with some bitterness, that even seemingly respectable families are quite inexplicably giving way on this point. Maybe it's a fact that many do it—or even that everyone does. But even if that's so, a bad thing remains bad even if everyone does it.

People say: 'The summer's so hot!' But there are fabrics on the market so light that they are perfectly suitable for wearing in the heat and can make garments just a little bit more ample. As for mixed groups and solitary car rides, it should come as no surprise to anyone that they are occasions of sin. 'My daughter's a good girl, she knows how to behave,' a lady told me. 'Your daughter is weak, as we all are,' I said, 'and should be protected against her own weakness and inexperience by being kept away from danger. Original sin is no myth, alas; it's a sad reality.'

After the sixth commandment comes the seventh. Some years ago a German bishop said that tourists should not be unfairly charged: a recommendation worth making. I've been told that in one of the mountain resorts the landscape is completed by a cow made of inflatable rubber. Seen from a distance, white against a green field, and with a large bell— also fake—round its neck, the cow adds a touch of colour to the scene and serves as an advertisement.

If this is true, then you could call it ingenious rather than tricky. But in some resorts, trickiness rather than ingenuity is the rule, and prices rocket during the holiday season. Some people consider holiday-makers only from the commercial point of view, as people with money to spend. It isn't always borne in mind that they're also people who have worked all the year in factories and offices, in damp, foggy cities; people who have just fifteen or twenty days in which to pause, and really do need rest and air and sun. It isn't always remembered—or it's not remembered enough—that they're our brothers, for whom we should feel warmth and charity, and to whom we ought to offer friendly hospitality.

St Peter recommended Christians to be hospitable among themselves, and added: 'without complaints.' Today we might add: 'without complaints or sharp practice!'

One final thought: *we* may go on holiday, but God doesn't.

Sunday is his day, and he wishes it to be kept unprofaned, both for his own honour and for our sake. When I say 'his day' I don't mean just the small part of it given over to the Mass we hear. The Christian Sunday is an entire day, which includes all kinds of things. It means the Mass or divine sacrifice, actively shared in, not merely listened to in a passive sort of way. It means caring for our souls quietly, by reflecting, by going to the sacraments. It means religious instruction, which we receive by listening to the priest and reading the Gospel or some oher good book. It means being in touch with the whole family of the parish. It means exercising charity towards the poor, the sick, and children. It means giving and receiving a good example. It is the reward, and the guarantee, of our good life.

If we can live well through Sunday, it's almost certain that we will live well through the rest of the week. This is why Our Lord is so anxious about his Sunday, and why we must do all we can not to let Sunday slip away. Tourism or no tourism, on public holidays or outside them, our souls are what matter more than anything else.

And now I'm back with you, Paolo Diacono. What do you think of my conclusion? Yes, it's old, but true and wise. It helps us to become good and to remain good, and this is all that matters.

GONZALO FERNANDEZ DE CORDOVA was the Spanish governor of the state of Milan during the war of Casale and the plague of 1630. He appears in Manzoni's *The Betrothed*, in which he deals with the Milanese uprising against his Commissioner of Supply, in which the hero of the novel, Renzo, was involved.

To Don Gonzalo Fernandez de Cordova

Dear Don Gonzalo,

All I know about you is the little Manzoni writes about you in *The Betrothed*. You were the Spanish governor of the state of Milan; the one in the war of Casale, and during the plague of 1630. In your coat-of-arms there was a Moorish king chained by the throat. It was when he was faced with that coat-of-arms at the Inn of the Full Moon, that Renzo burst out with: 'I know that heretic's face with a rope round its neck. . . . That face means, "Let those who can, give the orders, and those who want, obey them".'

Poor Renzo! It didn't go down too well, and a few hours later he had handcuffs put on him. He managed to escape but you pursued him furiously, calling him an 'evil character', a thief, and a seditious revolutionary!

Today, things would be very different.

For such a remark Renzo would be hailed as a prophet, a charismatic character, a theologian. The mere fact that you squawked in protest, dear Don Gonzalo, would make you into an oppressor, filled by a lust for power, trampling on human dignity and freedom.

The Milanese rising against your Commissioner of Supply would be called an insignificant failure, nothing in comparison with the true revolution that seeks to overthrow the system.

Today, certain philosophies and religious ways of thinking have sounded the death-knell for authority, and are all for freedom and revolution. They would make Bossuet, a genius who was almost your contemporary, say: 'Where everyone does what he wants, no-one does what he wants; where everyone gives orders, no-one gives orders.'

But who cares about Bossuet? The luminary very large numbers of students look to in particular is Mao, who has told them: 'Remove all that is bourgeois with the cultural revolution! The old-style culture only creates divisions. "Making the revolution" is the only culture worthy of the name.' This has been accepted in Italy, as well. The new students proclaim: 'We're the bomb that will blow up present-day society. No more selective schools, which favour only the bourgeoisie who have already had a particular type of education in the family! Away with the class-ridden meritocracy, which tries to measure the child who can go by car and the child who has to walk with the same standards at school.'

And they really mean it. They occupy the schools, and deny that there's any difference between Dante Alighieri and Bertoldini; they've learnt the methods of the urban guerrillas, the Marxist analysis of bourgeois society, and the use of drugs; they paralyse non-revolutionaries with ridicule, dominate the silent majority of students with terrorism, even penetrate the circles of Catholic students.

This is a curious phenomenon, a 'fifth column' that is accepted, applauded and seen in religious terms. Mao is the new Moses leading his people into a new Promised-Land. What is called Western democracy is now a useless ruin. Even Soviet communism has been superseded.

The third way, Mao's way, is the one that will free the world, because—they say—it's the way of the Gospel. How is that? Palestine in the time of Christ was a theatre of guerrilla war, they say. The guerrillas—the zealots—fought against Rome. The crucifixion was a reprisal against them, for the cross, before it became a Christian symbol, was a sign linked with guerrillas. Deprived of his rights as a citizen by the white colonialists from Rome, Jesus, a downtrodden Jew, couldn't fail to find himself among the revolutionaries.

This doesn't appear very clearly in the Gospels, they go on to say, because they were written when the revolt against Rome was over. Besides, St Mark was writing for the Romans and so watered down the contents of his Gospel and showed them in a better light. St Paul, a Roman citizen, let himself be influenced by Rome as well.

The Gospels and Epistles, then, must not be heeded, but must be re-interpreted.

It is written, 'Render to Caesar that which is Caesar's'. What should be written is: 'Give Caesar nothing, because everything in Palestine belongs to God.' It is written, 'Blessed are the peacemakers,' 'Go and be reconciled with your brother', 'Forgive one another', 'He who takes up the sword will perish by the sword', 'Turn the other cheek', 'Love your enemies'. These might seem to be pacifist texts, but in fact they are not. Understood in a pacifist sense, they sound absurd and cowardly to people longing for political independence under the oppressive yoke of Rome. So they should be re-interpreted as follows: No-one ought to have enemies, and this will be possible only when power has been overthrown by the revolution, and the devils of human indignity, economic disparity, and the disparity of power, which means oppression, have been destroyed.

The true Christ, they conclude, is a revolutionary and a guerrilla, who raised his hand against the merchants in the temple, and was in conflict with the synagogue. In order to follow him we must become revolutionaries against power, either state or ecclesiastical, in the name of freedom, co-responsibility, dialogue, and charisma.

* * *

What is one to say? Christ, though inferior to none, not even to the Father, was a model of respect towards human authority. At Nazareth he was subordinate to Mary and Joseph; at Capernaum he even worked a small miracle with the fishes in order to have the necessary means to pay the taxes in the Temple (Matthew 17). Christ's position in respect of the synagogue cannot be compared in the smallest way with ours in respect of the civil or ecclesiastical authorities. Christ was master of the law, son of the Father, superior to the law; the synagogue was merely the depository of the law. By coming up against the synagogue, Christ was not asserting the right to rebel; on the contrary, he was asserting his own right to obey the Father. Expelling the merchants from the Temple was a well-calculated, well-thought-out religious action. Christ didn't actually hurt or kill anyone, he didn't set the Temple on fire; he merely overturned the money-lenders' tables and scattered the merchants' animals, and caused not damage but momentary uneasiness, for an end he had considered in advance: he wished to teach them respect for his Father's house.

The Council emphasized that the Church is the people of God, and that it is a community rather than a hierarchy. In founding it, Christ had his people in mind, the souls to be saved, first of all. In order to serve the people he gave the Apostles and bishops special powers, and to keep the bishops united he established the Pope. The Pope and the bishops are not above the people of God, then; they are among them and at their service.

But they can serve only by exercising the powers they have been given. These cannot be abolished. The Council says: 'The bishops govern the particular churches confided to them as vicars or legates of Christ with advice, persuasion, example, but also with authority and sacred power ... by virtue of which they have the sacred right, and before God the duty, to give laws to their subjects, to judge and regulate everything that belongs to religion and the apostolate.'

Admittedly it is hard to exert authority in the right way. It is also true that the hierarchy may have been deficient in the past or may still in some ways be deficient: When the Fathers spoke of the 'leprous Church' or the 'lame Church', they were prodding a painful wound.

But this wound is connected with what is finite and human; and it can be cured, or made better, if not eliminated entirely. Laymen and priests who sometimes quarrel through sincere love of the Church should bear this in mind. We must learn to build on what exists: often it is wise to be content with what we have, at the same time trying to bring about improvements, while not destroying the chance of future development by fighting among ourselves.

Respect for people? Certainly, but the bishops cannot, out of respect for individuals, neglect the common good and allow indiscipline and anarchy. St Augustine said: 'We bishops are in charge, but only if we serve.' And he added: 'The bishop who fails to serve his people is merely a scarecrow stuck up in the vineyard to keep the birds from pecking at the grapes.'

More of the spirit, more charismatics, fewer institutions? But some of the institutions, such as the primacy of the Pope, the episcopal college, the episcopate, and the ministering priesthood, go back to Christ and cannot be touched without changing the very essense of the Church.

Other institutions are human, and should be changed when they are clearly superseded and counter-productive; but the laws of history must be followed. This tells the bishops: nothing human cannot be changed, even the Catholics' way of obeying. But it goes on: subjects must not think that the course of history can be hurried by impatience and rebelliousness. Bertoldino was in a hurry to bring the chicks to birth: he chased away the mother hen and took over from her himself, warming the eggs. But all he got was scrambled egg on his trousers!

More freedom, fewer legalistic ideas? Quite right. Christ proclaimed the inner life and condemned the legalistic attitudes of the Pharisees. St Paul also exalted freedom of the spirit and the code of love. But there is the other side of the coin: Christ laid down rules, which he made his followers obey, and wished to have authority in the Church. St Paul said: 'You have been called to freedom; but do not let this freedom become an excuse for the flesh.'

Co-responsibility? Our pastors remind us that they were not 'set up by Christ to bear alone the burden of the Church's saving mission'; 'in decisive battles, the best ideas often come from the front'. The laity, for its part, must not confine co-responsibility to protest, which is all too easy: it should make suggestions that are practical and achievable, and above all should collaborate in putting them into practice. People should remember, too, that their contribution to the good of the Church should not be made haphazardly, but 'under the guidance of the holy priesthood', whose special powers they must recognize and support.

Dialogue? The Council documents talk about it fifty times. It should be practised, then, with good will on both sides. The bishops should not listen only to themselves; they should consult with others and examine things together, before deciding. And the faithful should speak 'with the freedom and faith that belong to them as sons of God and brothers in Christ . . . always with truth, strength and prudence, with reverence and charity'.

But even dialogue won't work like a magic wand, curing and solving everything, putting everything in order. Dialogue is useful so long as those who use it trust it and keep to the rules.

* * *

Dear Don Gonzalo! These people, who say they are interpreting the Gospel, are seeking liberty. Alas, it was not the freedom Christ meant when he taught us to say: 'Father . . . deliver us from evil.'

Nor is it the other kind which St Augustine spoke of: 'You will be free, if you become a slave; free from sin, a slave of righteousness.'

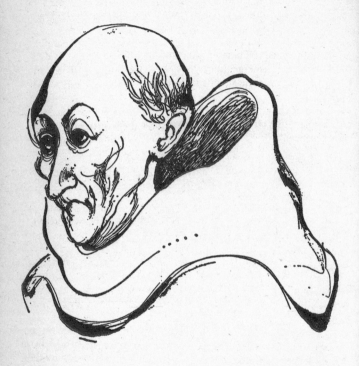

BERNARDINE OF SIENA, a saint of the Catholic Church (1380–1444), a Franciscan, and an exceptionally eloquent preacher, who left many works in Latin and Italian. In 1427 he put forward his 'seven rules' to the students of Siena University, which Cardinal Luciani advocates for the young people of today.

To St Bernardine of Siena

Dear smiling Saint,

Pope John liked your written sermons so much that he wanted to proclaim you a Doctor of the Church. He died, and nothing has so far been done about it. A pity!

What he liked best were not your sermons in Latin, carefully prepared, polished and subdivided, but those in Italian, collected from your spoken words and bursting with life, religious fervour, humour and practical wisdom. Perhaps he flattered you by calling you 'Smiling Doctor', together with the 'Mellifluous' Bernard, the 'Angelic' Thomas, the 'Seraphic' Bonaventure and the 'Consoling' Francis de Sales.

He thought that at a time when difficult words, full of cloudy 'isms', are used to express even the simplest things, it was the right time to draw attention to the friar who said: 'Speak clearly, so that whoever hears you goes away happy and enlightened, not confused.'

The teachers and students at the University of Siena in June 1427 certainly didn't go away confused by your teaching. You spoke of a 'way of studying,' suggested seven rules, and concluded: 'If you observe these seven rules and continue to do so, in a short time you will become a fine man or a fine woman.'

With your permission, I shall now try to recall your seven rules with today's students in mind, shortening them and making them a little more homely, as it were.

Today's students are nice, likeable people who are in no danger of being confused, for the simple reason that they want to experience things for themselves. They don't want 'models of behaviour', which smell of moralizing a mile off, either from you or from me. And probably they won't read this anyway. But I'll write it just the same; I'll write to you.

* * *

Rule one: *esteem*. No-one can study seriously if he doesn't first of all respect study. He can't become cultured if he doesn't first respect culture.

A student who loves studying will read a great deal. 'Good!' you write. 'Then you won't rot your brain like some youngsters, who don't study anything, but simply clutter up the lecture room benches.' Love books, and you'll be in touch with the great men of the past: 'you will speak to them, and they will speak to you: they will hear you, and you will hear them, and you will get great pleasure from it.'

What becomes of the student who won't work?

He becomes 'like a pig in a sty, who eats and drinks and sleeps.' He'll achieve nothing great or fine in life.

Of course, acquiring real culture involves more than reading: it means discussion, working in groups, exchanging experiences. All these things stimulate us to be active as well as receptive; they help us to be ourselves when we are learning, to show others our thoughts in an original way; they help us to treat our neighbour with courtesy and interest.

But we should never esteem the great ones of the past any the less. To receive great ideas from others is better than to invent mediocre ones ourselves. Pascal used to say: 'He who has climbed on to another's shoulders will see farther than the other, even if he is smaller than he is!'

* * *

Rule two: *detachment*. Detachment of oneself—at least a little— for without it no-one can study seriously. Athletes have to abstain from a great many things; the student is something of an athlete and you, dear brother Bernard, prepared a list of all 'forbidden' things.

I'll mention only two: bad company and bad reading. 'A libertine corrupts everyone,' you said. 'A bad apple, placed near good ones, corrupts the rest.' You tell students to beware even of the works of Ovid and 'other books about love'. Today you'd hardly touch on Ovid. Instead you would deal explicitly with indecent books and magazines, evil films and drugs. But you would stick to the following piece of advice. 'If you have a son studying at Bologna, or anywhere else, and hear that he is in love, don't send him any more money. Make him come home, because he won't learn a thing except songs and sonnets . . . and keep him close to you.'

This remedy really used to work: 'cutting off supplies'. But today it no longer works. The state takes over from Daddy if need be, by giving grants to university students.

One hope remains: that the student should apply the 'clown's cure' to himself. You know what it is: the clown is up on a chair with a crowd of gaping peasants around him on market day. He shows them a little closed box. 'In this,' he says, 'there's a wonderful cure for you if you're kicked by a mule. It costs very little, it's very cheap indeed, but it's a marvellous thing to have bought.' Plenty of those around him buy a box, and one of them opens his and finds nothing inside it but a couple of metres of thin string. 'It's a trick!' he yells furiously. 'That's no trick,' replies the trickster. 'You just keep as far away as the length of that string, and no mule's kick is ever going to reach you.'

This is the classic, radical remedy suggested by you preachers. And it works for everyone, particularly students, who are exposed to a thousand temptations. Detachment, separation—from all mules and their moral kicks!

* * *

Rule three: *quietness*. 'Our soul is like water. When it is still, the mind is like still water; but when it is moved, it becomes muddy.' So the mind needs to rest and be quiet, if it wishes to learn, deepen its learning and retain it. How can anyone fill his head with all the characters in magazines and films, on television and the world of sport—people who are so lively, so intrusive, and sometimes so depressing and corrupting—and then ask it also to retain the contents of his school books, which by comparison are so pale and colourless?

A band of silence is needed round the mind of anyone who is studying, to keep it quiet and clean. You, dear brother,

suggest asking God for it. You even suggest the right prayer: 'Lord, keep our minds quiet!' At this point our students may smile. But there it is: a touch of silence and a pinch of prayer in the midst of all our everyday uproar does no-one any harm.

* * *

Rule four: *order*, that is, balance and the right method, in both things of the body and those of the spirit. What about food? Yes, you write, but 'not too much or too little. All extremes are bad; the middle way is the best. You cannot bear two burdens: study and eating little, or eating too much and studying: the one will make you ill and the other will make your brain swell.' What about sleep? That too, 'not too much nor too little ... it is good to get up early ... with a sober mind.'

The spirit needs order too. 'Do not put the cart before the horse,' you continue. 'Learn less and know it well, rather than much which you know badly.' Things badly learned, superficiality, rough and ready methods—these aren't serious things. You also advise the student to go by his personal taste in choosing writers and subjects. 'One Doctor rather than another, one book rather than another, arouses more respect in you. ... But do not despise anyone.'

* * *

Rule five: *continuation*, which means perseverance. The fly alights on a flower and then flies on, restless and changeable; the hornet stops a little longer, but wants to buzz; the bee, though, is silent and busy, stops, sucks all the nectar, carries it home, and gives us the sweetest honey. St Francis de Sales wrote this and I think you will fully agree: you don't want students like flies or hornets, you like effective, tenacious will-power, and you are perfectly right.

In school and in life, it isn't enough to long for something, we must really wish it. It isn't enough to start wishing, we need to go on wishing. And it isn't even enough to go on wishing: we must know how to start again from the beginning every time we stop, through laziness, or failure, or collapse. A young student is unfortunate not so much if he has a bad memory as if he has a weak will. He is fortunate if he has, not so much a fine brain, as a strong tenacious will. But this is tempered only in the sun of God's grace, and warmed in the fire of great ideas and fine examples!

* * *

Rule six: *discretion*. This means suiting your aims to your ability. Don't get a crick in the neck gazing up at things too far above you. Don't try too many things at once. Don't expect results from one day to the next.

Think: it's nice to be first in class, but it's not for me if I haven't enough brains. I'll work as hard as I can and be pleased if I'm fourth or fifth. I'd like to learn to play the violin but I'll give up the idea if it harms my studies and makes people say: chasing two hares at once means losing both.

* * *

Rule seven: *enjoyment*, that is, a liking for study. No-one can go on studying for any length of time if he doesn't have a taste for it. And liking doesn't come all at once, it comes slowly. In the early stages there's always some obstacle: laziness to overcome, enjoyable occupations that attract us more, difficult subjects to deal with. Love of learning comes later, almost as a prize for the effort we've made. 'You don't have to go to Paris to study, you can learn from the ox, who eats and ruminates, a little at a time,' you wrote. To you, dear saint, 'ruminating' means rather more than chewing the cud. It means tasting the hay very slowly, when it is full of flavour and goodness. And this should happen with the books we learn from, which are the food of our minds.

* * *

Dear St Bernardine! Enea Silvio Piccolomini, your fellow citizen, who as pope took the name of Pius II, wrote that when you died the most powerful men in Italy divided your relics among them. The poor in Siena, who loved you so much, were left with nothing. All that was left was the ass on whose back you had sometimes ridden when you were tired in the last years of your life. One day the women of Siena saw the poor beast passing by, stopped it, shaved off all its hair, and kept the hairs as relics.

I have shaved, not the ass, but one of your wonderful sermons, and have pulled out what I can from it. Will these relics of it be scattered to the four winds, or will some of them at least be gathered up by someone?

St Francis de Sales, a Catholic preacher and Doctor of the Church (1567–1622), who studied with the Jesuits in Paris and then at Padua University, where he took his degree in civil law. He became a priest, then Bishop of Geneva, where he undertook the conversion of the Calvinists. He is celebrated for his work with children, the sick and the poor, and he wrote various spiritual books, among them *Introduction to the Devout Life* and *Treatise on the Love of God*.

To St Francis de Sales

Gentlest of saints,

I have re-read a book about you: *St Francis de Sales and our heart of flesh*. It was written by Henry Bordeaux of the French Academy.

First, though, you yourself wrote that you had a 'heart of flesh,' a tender, understanding heart that bore in mind the fact that men were not pure spirits, but sensitive beings. With this human heart of yours you loved literature and the arts, wrote with the most delicate sensibility, and even encouraged your friend Bishop Camus to write novels. You bent down over everyone, and gave each person something.

When you were a university student in Padua you made a rule that you would never run away or cut short a conversation with anyone, however dislikeable and boring; that you would be modest without insolence, easy-going without austerity, gentle without affectation, and yielding without opposition.

And you kept your word. To your father, when he chose a rich, pretty heiress as your bride, you replied pleasantly: 'Father, I've seen the young lady, and she deserves better than me!'

As priest, missionary and bishop you gave your time to others: to children, the poor, the sick, sinners, heretics, the middle classes, noblewomen, prelates, princes.

Like everyone else, you were misunderstood and contradicted; your 'heart of flesh' suffered, but you continued to love your opponents. 'If someone, in hatred, were to pluck out my left eye,' you said, 'I think I could look kindly at him with my right one. If he plucked that one out too, I would still have my heart with which to love him.'

Many would call this the summit of achievement. But you thought the summit was elsewhere. 'Man is the perfection of the universe,' you wrote; 'the spirit is the perfection of man; love is the perfection of the spirit; the love of God is the perfection of love.' So the summit of achievement, the perfection and excellence of the universe, were, to you, loving God.

* * *

You therefore believed in the primacy of God's love. Was it a matter of making people good? Let these people begin by loving God. Once this love was lit in their hearts, and established there, the rest would follow of its own accord.

Modern treatment of illness says you can't cure a local malady if you don't achieve health in the whole body by generally good hygiene and a powerful restorative such as a blood transfusion. This is similar to what you wrote: 'The lion is a powerful animal, and very resourceful,' you said. 'For this reason it can sleep without fear in a hidden den or on the side of a road used by other animals.' And you concluded that we should all become spiritual lions, full of strength and the love of God, and therefore unafraid of other animals without these things.

According to you, this was St Elizabeth of Hungary's system. This queen used to go to balls and other entertainments at court, and instead of being harmed by them she gained spiritual advantages from being there. Why? Because 'in the wind [of temptation] large fires [of divine love] are spread further, whereas small fires are put out.'

Lovers in this world of ours say: 'Love and a hut!' Later, when love has grown cold, they find a hut isn't enough, and they don't want to stay there.

You wrote: 'As soon as the queen bee goes out into the fields, all her people surround her; thus the love of God does not enter into a heart without a whole crowd of other virtues taking up residence there.' To you, preaching about virtue to a heart without the love of God was like suggesting that someone with a weak body should suddenly take up athletics. Strengthening the organism with the love of God, on the other hand, means training a champion and launching him confidently up to the heights of saintliness.

* * *

But what kind of a love of God? One kind consists of sighs, and pious groans, and eyes turned sweetly to heaven. Another is masculine and frank, and like the love that possessed Christ when he said, in the garden, 'Not my will, but thine be done'. This is the only kind of love of God you recommended.

According to you, those who love God must embark on God's ship, having decided to accept the route chosen by their captain, through the orders of those who represent him and the situations and circumstances of life which he allows.

You imagined interviewing Marguerite when she was about to embark for the East with her husband Louis IX, King of France.

'Where are you going, your Majesty?'

'Wherever the king goes.'

'But do you know exactly where the king is going?'

'He has told me in a general way, but I'm not anxious to know, I only want to go with him.'

'So, your Majesty, you have no idea about this journey?'

'No, I have no idea, except that it will be in the company of my dear lord and husband.'

'Your husband is going to Egypt, and stopping at Acre, and many other places. Don't you mean to go there too, your Majesty?'

'No, not really. All I want is to be near my king. It is quite unimportant to me where he goes, except in so far as he will be there. I'm not so much going as following him. I don't want to make this journey, but the king's presence is enough for me.'

The king is God, and we are Marguerite, if we seriously love God. And how many times, and in how many ways, did you return to this idea! 'With God, we should feel like a child in its mother's arms,' you wrote. 'If he carries us on the left arm or the right, it is all the same to us, we let him do what he wants.' Suppose the Madonna handed the infant Jesus over to a nun? Someone asked you this, and you replied: 'The sister wouldn't want to give him back, but she would be wrong. Old Simeon received the Child in his arms with joy, but soon gave him

back with joy. In the same way we need not mind giving up our responsibilities, our job, our office, when our time is up and we are asked to do so.'

In God's house we must try to accept any job: cook or kitchen boy, waiter, stable boy, baker. If it pleases the king to call us into his private council, then we must go there, but without being too excited, for we know that our reward depends not on the job itself but on the faithfulness with which we serve him.

This was what you thought. Some people have considered it a kind of Eastern-style fatalism. But it was not. 'Human will,' you wrote, 'is the master of its affections, as a girl is in command of the suitors who ask for her hand in marriage. That is, before she has made her choice; but once she has chosen and has become a married woman, the situation is turned round: she is no longer in command but has become a subject, and remains subject to him who was once her prey. The will can choose whatever love it wants, but once it has chosen a particular allegiance, it belongs there. But the will has a freedom which the married woman has not, for it can reject its love whenever it wants to, even the love of God.' This cancels out any idea of fatalism.

*　　*　　*

If only the politicians could hear you! They measure any action by its success. 'Does it succeed? Then it's right.' Whereas you said: 'An action is right, even if it does not succeed, when it is carried out for the love of God. The merit of the cross we carry lies not in its weight but in the way we carry it. There may be more merit in carrying a small cross made of straw than a large one made of iron. Eating, drinking and walking, if done for the love of God, may be worth more than fasting or lashes from a whip.' But you took another step forward by saying that the love of God may, in a way, actually change things, making a good thing out of an action which in itself is neither good nor bad, or may even be dangerous. This was so with games of chance and dancing (the kind known in your day, of course) if they were used for enjoyment and not through attachment; for a little while, and not to the point where one was tired and dizzy; and rarely, so that they did not become an occupation rather than a recreation.

It is the quality of our actions that we should consider, then, rather than their size and number. Did you read what Rabelais, who was almost a contemporary of yours, wrote about the devotions taught to the young Gargantua? 'Twenty-seven or thirty masses to hear every day, a series of Kyrie eleisons that would have been enough for sixteen hermits!' You may or may not have read him, but you certainly gave the right answer when you taught your nuns: 'It is right to go ahead, but not with too many pious practices. Perfect the few you already have. Last year you fasted three times a week; this year you want to double the fast, and can still fit that into a week. But what about next year? If you want to add your original fasts yet again, will you make it nine times a week or twice a day? Be careful! It is madness to wish to die a martyr in the Indies, and neglect the duties of every day.'

In other words: don't so much practise devotions as *have devotion*. The soul is not so much a cistern to be filled as a fountain that must be made to play.

*　　*　　*

And not only the souls of nuns. When these principles are applied, sanctity ceases to be a privilege of convents and becomes the power and the duty of all. This doesn't make it an easy task (it is the way of the cross!), but it does mean that it is an ordinary one: some people achieve it with heroic actions or vows—and are like eagles, flying high in the heavens; many achieve it by following the common duties of every day, but in an uncommon way, like doves, flying from roof to roof, close to the ground.

Why long for the flight of an eagle, for the desert, for a harsh severe cloister, if you are not called to them? Let us not behave like neurotic invalids who long for cherries in autumn and grapes in spring. Let us apply what God asks of us according to the state in which we find ourselves. 'Madame,' you wrote, 'you must cut down your prayers a little, to avoid neglecting your duties in the home. You are married; be a wife completely, without too much modesty; do not annoy your family by shutting yourself up in church too much; make your piety the kind that will make your husband love it too. But this will happen only if he feels you are his.'

* * *

This, then, is the ideal of the love of God, lived in the midst of the world: that these men and these women should have wings to fly to God with loving prayer; that they should also have feet to walk pleasantly with others; and that they should have, not gloomy faces, but smiling ones, knowing they are going to the happy house of the Lord.

THE LEGENDARY BEAR who ate St Romedio's horse was tamed and bridled and became the inseparable companion of the hermit, who had been Count of Thaur, near Innsbruck, and then become an anchorite in the Val di Non near Sanzeno in the fourth century.

To St Romedio's Bear

Dear Bear of St Romedio,

'Every Good Thief has his followers.' And this is why a month ago, as I went through Sanzeno in Val de Non, I said to myself: 'A couple of kilometres from here, at the bottom of a small valley, enclosed between very high rocks that make you think of the Grand Canyon, is the sanctuary of St Romedio. Your grandparents walked miles to go there. You're in a car— why not go too?' And so I went.

The sanctuary, consisting of six superimposed churches and of the terrace that looks out over the great drop in the landscape, is interesting. So are the statue and relics of the lonely hermit. But you, dear Bear, are very likeable too!

The statue by Perathoner shows you held on a lead by the saint, and looking very gentle and tame. They told me all about you. According to the legend, when he was on his way back from a pilgrimage to Rome, Romedio stopped to rest with his two faithful companions, Abraham and David. After a while he said to David: 'It's time to get back onto the road. Go and fetch our horses in the field.' David went off, then came back terrified: a bear was eating Romedio's horse. Romedio rushed into the field, saw what was happening, and said quite calmly to you: 'Bear! Obviously you're hungry as you're eating my horse. That's all very well, but I can't walk home, you know, so you'll have to be my horse.' And he put the saddle, bridle and reins of the horse you had eaten on to you, climbed on to your back as if you were the most peaceable mule in the world, and set off in the direction of Trento. When I left the sanctuary, my prayer was (can you believe it?): 'Tame me, Lord! Make me more helpful and less of a bear!'

Don't be upset by this last expression of mine. Brown or black bears, with long bodies, short legs and thick coarse pelts, seem clumsy, inelegant creatures to us men. We consider ourselves infinitely attractive, slim and graceful by comparison. If

133

you try dancing it's a disaster, whereas our dancers are miracles of musical grace and those in our ballet so light and agile that they could dance on the flowers of the field without crushing them.

* * *

Well, what of it? Yesterday I was tempted to turn my month-old prayer right round and say: 'Lord, make us all become bears!' What happened was that I overheard some ugly swearing. 'What does it matter whether we dress elegantly,' I thought, 'whether we wear fine shoes, and ties in the latest fashion, and do our hair so beautifully, if words as filthy as these come out of our mouths? Better to be clumsy like bears, and not have dirty minds!'

This is particularly true in Italy, where swearing is so widespread it has become a real epidemic. Fifteen million Italians regularly swear, producing about a billion oaths a day.

Some of these are psychologically like Dante's 'grim, contemptuous' Capaneo, who hurls proud oaths of defiance and scorn at God. Others water down their blasphemous expressions a little. 'Is there still a God?' they say. 'Stop telling me about a God who's good and just.' 'Religion is nothing but a big shop.' 'The devil knows more than God.'

Luckily the hearts of those who say these things aren't always in agreement with their voices and for a number of reasons they don't really and profoundly mean to offend God.

Sometimes the seriousness of what they say is diminished by thoughtlessness, worry or ignorance. This happened to Irene Papovna, who turned up to take a competitive exam in Moscow. She was told: 'Analyse the inscription carved on Lenin's tomb.' She couldn't quite remember what it was, but thought—though she wasn't sure—that it was something like 'Religion is the opium of the people'. What on earth was she to do? She took the risk, analysed the inscription she thought she had remembered and as soon as she had finished rushed out into Red Square, in front of the Lenin Mausoleum, to check it. Finding she had hit on the right inscription she let out a glad cry: 'Dear, good God! And dear holy Virgin of Kazan! Thank you for having made me remember it!'

* * *

Dear Bear! You don't know it, but there's now a whole dictionary on swearing and bad language. This is agreed and accepted, realistic and vivid, if not always well chosen.

Oaths, for instance, are known as *candles*. But candles give light, whereas an oath is a black word, stagnant water, poison gas. Women's swearing is called 'Washerwomen's language'. This isn't really fair to washerwomen. It might just as well be called school mistresses' language, or girl students' language, or women workers' language, or typists' language, or anything else like that. It used to be said of all these women: 'They blush, if they're embarrassed.' Today you'd have to say of some of them: 'They're embarrassed if they blush.'

People also say that someone 'swears like a Turk', but that's calumny: the Turks don't swear. In France, though, and in Switzerland and Germany, they say (with reason, alas): 'He swears like an Italian.'

* * *

It's a widespread illness, then. What's the diagnosis?

The first symptom is great superficiality. The man who reasons doesn't swear and the man who swears doesn't reason. Either this God they swear at exists or else he doesn't. If he doesn't, then there's no point in swearing at him; if he does, then swearing at him is insane, because 'a donkey's bray doesn't reach the sky'. Other sins can be understood (not excused): the thief, after all, gets his hands on a wallet full of money; the drunkard gets his on a bottle of good wine; but what does the person who swears get his hands on?

The second symptom is a poor sense of responsibility. There's not just God to consider: there's his neighbour. You, dear Bear, who were famous for the tenderness you showed towards your children, should say to fathers of families: 'When you swear, you upset your wife and little daughter, and shock your son, who's encouraged to follow your example. What do you gain from that?'

'This is what I gain,' I can hear the blasphemer say. 'When I swear, I'm protesting against things that are going wrong. I toughen up my speech, let my anger burst out.'

Protests? When they're useful and rational, they should be made. But does your car engine which isn't working start up the moment you begin taking it out on God?

Toughening up your speech? Right, so long as you stick to inoffensive phrases. Plenty can be found that are both innocent and dynamic. A nice Australian parish priest demonstrated this to some peasants one fine day, when he turned up in a field, picked up the plough, cracked the whip and roared at the oxen: 'Up with you, my sweet archangels! That's it, you lovely cherubim! Get a move on, you flaming seraphim!' At these mystical, celestial orders the oxen slowly rose and, though puzzled, began to pull the plough.

As for anger, if it's a fact that we ought to control our passions and not be subject to them, then we ought to repress it, not let it burst out.

* * *

Any diagnosis must be followed by treatment. A good poultice in a case like ours, dear Bear, may be a moderate, well-chosen reaction.

A monk much like your St Romedio was in a railway carriage listening to a pair of impolite youngsters trying to outdo each other in bad language. It upset him, but he felt he could do nothing. Then one of the boys spoke to him: 'Father, I've got some bad news for you,' he said, 'the devil's died.' 'Oh really?' said the monk. 'I'm most awfully sorry. My sincere condolences to you both.' 'Condolences?' the boys cried. 'Whatever for?' 'Because I'm so sorry for you, left as orphans like this!'

The monk had allowed himself a pinch of irony. But we oughtn't really to feel ironical about those who swear, especially the young. We should show interest, understanding, a wish to help; and we should offer to do so. We may be their companions or their friends, their superiors or their relations; well, tactfully and delicately, and with respect for each personality, we should— depending on our relationship with each—give them friendly advice, or remonstrate politely, or scold them, or sometimes even punish them.

The real remedy, though, is for them to make a firm decision to give up the bad habit, and then stick to it.

* * *

Dear Bear! Open your jaws wide and, from your sanctuary, say this as loudly as you can to all Italians!

PAVIL IVANOVIC CHICHIKOV is the disreputable hero of Gogol's *Dead Souls* who makes a fortune as the result of a gigantic swindle. Nikolai Gogol (1809–52) is one of the most popular figures in Russian literature, a pitiless observer of Russian society with great psychological subtlety and sensitivity. *Dead Souls* (1842) is acclaimed as one of the greatest novels in the Russian language, notable for its characterization, humour and style.

To Pavel Ivanovic Chichikov

Dear Mr Chichikov,

The visiting card you left with the servant when you came to the hotel gives you a rank equivalent to that of colonel in the Tsarist army.

Gogol describes you as being not handsome but not ugly either; not too fat nor too thin; not old, but not very young.

You had a masterpiece of a plan in your mind, though, which you were about to carry out. You had been told: 'The government is handing out land to be colonized near Cherson to anyone who shows that he has a fair number of farm servants or "souls". A short time ago there was an epidemic and many serfs died there, thanks be to God; but they still appear on the registers as if they were alive.' I'm going to profit from this, you thought. I'll buy them from their owners as 'live souls', even if they're really 'dead souls', present my list to the government, and so obtain land and become immensely rich.

Having left your luggage at the hotel, you set off at once on visits round the town.

To the governor you mentioned—just in passing, of course—that entering his territory was like entering paradise, that the streets were like velvet, that the government deserved a monument for sending out such intelligent public servants.

To the chief of police you said something very flattering about the local policemen.

In talking to the assistant governor and the local magistrate you let slip the title of 'Excellency'. It was a mistake, but pleased them both a great deal.

The result was that the governor invited you to a small family gathering that evening, and the others expected you during the next few days: some for lunch, some for a game of cards, some for a cup of tea. Already you were on the crest of the wave, Chichikov, your outsize lie seemed all set to prosper and

139

you were about to make a fortune at the expense—of course—of others.

This is the sad thing about it. You're a clever fellow and have had an original idea, but ... it's a swindle! And what's worse, as you're an amusing swindler who wears gloves, society's all over you and pays you compliments.

If only you were the only one! But there's any number of others. There's Talleyrand, who calls words a gift of God 'to hide what we really think'; or Byron, who wrote: 'And after all, what is a lie? 'Tis but the truth in masquerade'; or Ibsen, who in *The Wild Duck* defends the 'vital lie', saying that ordinary men need lies in order to live; or Andreev, who in *The Lie* says sadly that there's no longer any truth. And so we come on to the practical application of all this by many who think tricks and deceit are a proof of intelligence and of ability in business.

*　　*　　*

Today, alas, we have even more enormous cases, made possible by new techniques of communication, which you, Chichikov, couldn't even have imagined. Today these are exploited by the few in order to harm a great many.

Gilbert Cesbron has recently produced a new psychological novel. It may interest you, great impostor, to know that he called it *This is the Time of Impostors*.* Cesbron's impostors are those who use the national press to put out scandals and calumnies, to make indiscreet insinuations and play on people's worst instincts, thus gradually undermining their moral sense.

To the national press, Cesbron might have added the cinema, radio and television. These new instruments, which in themselves are very useful, can make children hate the best of fathers, and see white as black or vice versa, if they're cunningly manoeuvred. This means using screen and sound-track in the most persuasive way possible, in secret ways that are amazingly effective.

Your lies, Chichikov, with the appropriate smiles and seductive compliments, could be multiplied a thousand times today and become a choral lie—national, international, and cosmic—

**Ecco il tempo degli impostori*

making ours the real 'time of impostors', as Cesbron puts it.

What's more, through the press, radio and television we seldom come into contact with the facts themselves, only with a version of the facts, interpreted in a great many different ways. The pernicious idea that we can never arrive at the truth, but only at an opinion, then creeps into the mind. 'Once there were certainties,' people say to themselves, 'now we're no longer in the age of belief, but in the age of opinion.'

Philosophers fan the flames. 'Language,' they say, 'isn't suited to the expression of thought. Truth is relative; that is, it changes according to the times and the people involved.' This explains why many people have no trust in the truth, in human reason, or in the strength of logic; this makes them content to abandon themselves to mere impressions—illogically and un-critically.

What's false to one is true to another. Truth and lies are given equal rights of citizenship. This is a real blow to the dignity of man and the goodness of God, who has created man capable of certainties. It wouldn't matter so much if we stopped in the natural field, but we go into the religious field and the divine.

People say: 'We're all cripples in the face of truth. Authori-tative teaching was at one time found in the Church. Now we're all seeking it. It's the age of pluralism in faith.'

But faith isn't pluralistic; we can admit a healthy pluralism in theology, in the liturgy, in all kinds of other things, but never in faith. As soon as it's known that God has revealed a truth, the answer is *yes*, for everyone, at all times; *yes* with conviction and courage, without doubts and hesitations.

And we must reject with all our strength the idea that the truths of the faith are merely expressions of a moment in the consciousness and in the life of the Church. They are right for ever, even though it's possible to come to a better understanding of them and to express them with new formulas, better conceived and better adapted to modern times.

As for authoritative teaching, it has always been there—within the right limits—and will continue to be. The Church would otherwise cease to be apostolic, and it would no longer be true that 'Jesus Christ [is] the same yesterday, and today and for ever' (Heb., 13, 8).

Unlike these doubters and sceptics, Chichikov, you continue to conduct your affairs with perfect self-confidence. Without batting an eyelash you fire out figures, give assurances, remove obstacles. There are people like you in their undaunted confidence who think themselves gifted with the power of prophesy, point the finger, and keep denouncing other people and institutions.

· 'Prophetic denunciation' is the literary *genre* put forward today by some people in the Catholic Church. There's no doubt that it's often used with good intentions, and a love for the Church. The scandal provoked by the denunciation is often deliberately unleashed: 'Some people need to have guns fired to make them wake up!' St Paul preferred to say: 'If a food scandalizes one of my brothers, I will never eat meat again.'

The saints, Chichikov, even those turned out in your Russia, like St Nicholas, went another way, as a rule: they stood up to themselves rather than to others, and were always afraid of sinning against charity.

Magdalen de Lamoignon, a noble, cultivated Sister of Charity in the seventeenth century, read the satires of the poet Boileau and found them too vicious. She told the author so frankly. 'I'll be careful to remember what you've said another time,' said Boileau. 'But at least allow me to write against the Grand Turk, who's a bitter enemy of the Church.' 'Oh no,' replied the nun. 'He's a sovereign and should be respected for the authority he embodies.' 'Let me at least write a satire against the devil,' said Boileau, smiling. 'You won't deny he deserves it.' 'The devil's been punished enough already,' said the nun. 'Let's try not to speak ill of anyone. That way we won't run the risk of going out to look for it.'

Was it to avoid that risk, perhaps, that everyone believed in you, Chichikov? Others haven't your luck: they're not believed even when they tell the truth.

This happened to the soldier who was wounded in the leg

and begged a fellow soldier to take him to the field hospital. On the way there a cannon-ball neatly whisked off the man's head, without his helper noticing. When he reached the hospital with his burden he heard the surgeon say: 'What d'you think I can do to a man without a head?' Only then did the helpful soldier look at the body and exclaim: 'You dirty liar! You told me you were wounded in the leg!'

There's a middle way. This means neither blind, unlimited trust in other people's every word and action, nor exaggerated suspiciousness that thinks everyone is deceiving us, even if there's no reason for it.

Blind faith was avoided by the police inspector who arrested two men he saw wearing overalls and loading lead pipes onto a lorry. 'What made you think they were thieves and not workmen?' he was asked. 'They were working too fast to be workmen,' he replied.

Exaggerated suspiciousness wasn't avoided, though, by the doctor who said to his colleague: 'I won't make you a loan because I don't trust anyone. If St Peter were to come down from heaven and ask me for a small loan, getting the Blessed Trinity to sign a guarantee, I still wouldn't give him anything.' Mark Twain was also suspicious. 'Never tell lies,' he wrote in the album of a young lady who had been badgering him to do so; and added: 'except to keep in training.'

* * *

Mr Chichikov, Gogol says that before you finally prepared to carry out your enormous deception you didn't fail to make the sign of the cross, Russian-style. Before starting off on your lie, you called on Him who 'came to bear witness to the truth' (John, 18, 37), who is the truth and said: 'Let your communication be, Yea, yea; nay, nay' (Matthew, 5, 37). You put truth and lies together with an incredible degree of incongruity. This is the saddest aspect of your lying.

We who are seeking an authentic Christianity must try and do the opposite of what you did. We stand for a life without deceit and double dealing. And I say this with no bitterness!

LEMUEL, King of Massa, is named in the Bible (Proverbs 31) as the author of the famous poem in praise of the ideal woman. Nothing else is known about him. Some critics have, without much basis, suggested that he was in fact Solomon.

To Lemuel, King of Massa

Dear Lemuel,

The Bible names you as the author of the famous poem in praise of the ideal woman. Nothing else is known about you.

May I say, though, that you took the opposite position to that of Cornelia, mother of the Gracchi. She showed her sons to her women friends and said: 'These are my jewels.' You turned things round by showing a mother and saying: 'Her children arise up, and call her blessed; her husband also, and he praiseth her.'

Well, one thing's certain: your splendid song of praise certainly seems applicable to our own time, when we hear so much about the advancement of women.

Do you know, the other day a little schoolgirl made me quite embarrassed by saying: 'Is it right for Our Lord to have made seven sacraments, but only six for women?' She was referring, of course, to Holy Orders, which has always been reserved for men.

What could I reply? I looked round and said: 'I can see boys and girls in this class. Now, can any of you boys say: "Only one man on earth was the father of Jesus?"' 'No, because St Joseph was only his foster father,' the boys replied. 'But can you girls say to me "A woman was Jesus's mother".' 'Yes,' said the girls. 'Quite right,' I said. 'Now, consider this. There may not be women popes or women bishops or women priests, but the motherhood of God makes up for this a thousand times over, and honours all women, and motherhood itself as well.'

The little girl seemed persuaded.

The magnificent praises in your song have been contrasted by some people with St Paul's so-called shabbiness in saying: 'Let your women keep silent in the churches' (1 Cor. 14, 34).

My own view is that St Paul meant this to apply only to the women of Corinth and only at that particular time. In Corinth just then there was a remarkable upsurge of charismatics, both men and women; and, at the meetings, these people would get up to speak or to pray, filled with the Spirit of the Lord. Some women got up without being true charismatics, and this caused confusion and uneasiness. In order to avoid this being repeated, St Paul decided to forbid all women to speak in that particular congregation.

A little earlier, in the same letter to the Corinthians, he had recognized that women could prophesy, so long as they did so with their heads covered.

Once, when he was in Caesarea, he spent several days with St Luke in the house of Philip, a deacon and missionary, making no objection when Philip's four daughters 'prophesied' (Acts 21, 8–9). Finally, in his last years, he recommended Titus to instruct old women, because they were 'teachers of good things that they may teach the young women' (Titus 2, 3–4).

Besides, didn't the prophet Joel announce solemnly that in the time of the Messiah the daughters as well as the sons of Israel would prophesy (Joel 2, 28–29)? And, in the days of Pentecost, didn't St Peter declare that the prophecy of Joel was coming true and the Lord was pouring out his spirit upon his servants and handmaids (Acts 2, 18)?

Even before the coming of Christ prophecy wasn't denied to women. Priests have always been exclusively male, but the mantle of prophecy was sometimes laid on the shoulders of women.

Miriam, the sister of Moses and Aaron, directed the songs of the women during a religious celebration, carrying a tambourine (Ex. 15, 20); she was known as a prophetess and later called the people to witness that 'the Lord [had] indeed spoken [by her]' (Numbers 12, 2). Deborah, in the time of Judge Barak, was a kind of Joan of Arc, or rather a Peter the Hermit in petticoats, who preached a holy war and foretold certain victory. On Mount Ephraim, under 'the palm tree of Deborah', she sat while 'the children of Israel came up to her for Judgement' (Judges 4, 5). The high priest Hilkiah, 621 years before Christ, went with other distinguished people, on orders from King Josiah, to consult the prophetess Huldah '. . . [who] dwelt in Jerusalem in the college'. And the prophetess began speaking exactly as the prophets did: 'Thus saith the Lord' (2 Kings 22, 14–16). Even Anna, the widow of eighty-four who approached the infant Jesus when he was brought to the Temple and went about speaking of him, was called a prophetess (Luke 2, 36–39).

*　　*　　*

Your ideal woman, King Lemuel, is hard-working, tireless, a real Martha: 'She girdeth her loins with strength, and strengtheneth her arms . . . She riseth also while it is yet night . . . Her candle goeth not out by night.'

And her work fills her with joy: 'She worketh wool and flax, and worketh willingly with her hands . . . She perceiveth that her merchandise is good . . . and she shall rejoice in time to come.' This reveals another quality: gaiety, sister of goodness, tenderness, labour and love.

A husband needs that cheerful serenity when he comes home tired from his work. The children need it too, since joy provides the right atmosphere for any system of education that is to thrive. Maintaining this gaiety at all costs, even on bad days; showing it even when endless, minute, monotonous physical labour seems to break a woman's back and bring tears into her eyes— this is indeed a great virtue. In fact it is Christian fortitude, a form of penitance that, under certain conditions, may be like the sacrifices and long prayers of monks and nuns. This doesn't prevent your ideal woman, King Lemuel, from being far-sighted and sharp-witted: 'She considereth a field, and buyeth it; with the fruit of her hand she planteth a vineyard . . . She maketh fine linen, and selleth it; and delivereth girdles unto the merchant.' You certainly can't say her home lacks leadership, and it's clear why her husband has trustfully handed over to her the keys of the cellar and the cupboards, quite sure that everything will be kept in good order. This husband is like King Malcolm of Scotland who, though he was illiterate, used to kiss the prayer-book of his holy wife Margaret; the book, he said, that made her so wise and so good!

* * *

Your ideal woman is socially aware of things: 'She stretcheth out her hand to the poor; yea, she reacheth forth her hand to the needy.' Her servants and handmaidens are made to work, but she outdoes them in their labours and sees they lack nothing they need. In a hard winter she brings out warm clothes, 'for all her household are clothed in scarlet'.

Today, King Lemuel, justice and social charity are dealt with in a very different way. Our women are more often employed as working dependants than they are as mistresses of a household. They now hold every kind of position in politics, administration and the world of work, and no praise is handed out to the woman who simply cares for her home.

In your day, the children, the whole family, were protected within the home. Today they are protected outside it: in the electoral voting booth, in the trade unions, in all kinds of organisations. Even nuns must know how to exploit their new civil liberties to the utmost, and women who occupy public positions must be able to carry out their duties like men, while using the diligence, tact, delicacy and care that belong, in particular, to their sex.

If Napoleon, who disliked hearing women talk about politics, were alive today, as he was in the middle of the Terror, he would find not one but thousands of women to tease him as Madame de Stael did. 'General,' she said, 'the Republic today beheads women. So women should at least have the right to ask why they are being beheaded.'

Your song, it has been remarked, scarcely mentions conjugal love. Some Catholics writers today, in speaking of the ideal woman, would give a great deal more space to the subject. Your method is preferable, though; it shows the sort of prudence of which Manzoni gave a Christian example in *The Betrothed*.

The love of Renzo and Lucia, who are engaged, is pure, virtuous and delicate. When Lucia stays with Donna Prassede, she avoids talking of her troubles, being too embarrassed to use the only word that applies to her feelings—that is, the word 'love'. She is surprised and embarrassed, too, when faced with the probing questions of the nun Gertrude; at other times she blushes, and in the *lazzaretto's* hut Renzo seeks her eyes in vain.

On the night of the flight, when Renzo gets out of the boat to land, he gives his hand to Agnese but, out of delicacy, fails to take Lucia's. A little earlier, 'Lucia clung close to her mother's arm, gently but adroitly avoiding the help which the young man offered her in the difficult parts of that cross-country journey, feeling ashamed, even in this trouble, of having been alone with him so long and on such familiar terms when she had expected to become his wife a few moments afterwards.'

Such delicacy and prudence are found in the novels of Sir Walter Scott, too. The man who is courting the Fair Maid of Perth, for instance, complains to his future father-in-law of her extreme reserve. 'I believe she thinks the whole world is one great minster-church, and that all who live in it should behave as if they were at an eternal mass,' he says.

Perhaps the Fair Maid of Perth exaggerated a little, but our permissive society exaggerates the other way. I should say it does!

*　　*　　*

Your ideal woman is entirely dedicated to the family; she breathes goodness and spreads it around her. 'She opens her mouth with wisdom; and her tongue is the law of kindness. . . . The heart of her husband doth safely trust in her.' Thanks to her, 'her husband is known in the gates, when he sitteth among the elders of the lands'.

This reminds me of Pope Sixtus V, who said: 'Show me a woman whose husband has never complained of anything, and I will canonize her at once.' A woman like that is not merely a saint within her own family; she draws her husband and children up with her. When I heard that the parents of St Theresa of Lisieux were being considered for beatification, I said: 'At last, a couple are being considered! St Louis IX is a saint without his Margaret, St Monica is one without her Patrick. But Zélie Guérin will be a saint with Louis Martin her husband, and with Theresa her daughter.'

* * *

The ideal woman, as you said, King Lemuel, likes elegance, grace and comfort. 'She maketh herself coverings of tapestry; her clothing is silk and purple . . . strength and honour are her clothing.' But then you add at once: 'favour is deceitful, and beauty is vain; but a woman who feareth the Lord, she shall be praised.'

Beauty is one of God's gifts; the art of dressing with taste and elegance is praiseworthy, especially in a woman; and even cosmetics are not, in many cases, things to be disapproved of. But they are all passing things. To be a friend of God, to be close to him in a good life and in sincere religious feeling, is far more secure and lasting. And it is this closeness that should be cultivated with the other qualities—and more than them.

Maria Cristina of Savoy, when she was the young, attractive and cultivated queen of Naples, wrote about this in a poem: poem:
I am healthy, rich and fair, but what of it?
I have gold and silver, but what of it?
I am almost unequalled in my wit and knowledge, but what of it?
Were I to enjoy the world for a thousand years, what of it?
Death comes to all, and nothing remains:
Serve God, and you will have everything later!

This young queen's thought may seem a little sad. But it is undoubtedly true, King Lemuel.

SIR WALTER SCOTT (1771–1832), an enthusiastic collector of the popular traditions of Scotland, and the pioneer of the historical novel (*Ivanhoe, Kenilworth, Quentin Durward*) envisaged as an exciting story of national events, yet based upon serious research. He was very much imitated and, as the initiator of a new genre, influenced the rest of European literature.

To Sir Walter Scott

Dear Sir Walter,

How many novels did you write? In your lifetime they had enormous success. Today people don't read them very often, but when I was a boy I loved them. I liked your simple, unstuffy manner, your ability to create characters, and the art with which you set them against a historical background—sometimes in the Middle Ages, sometimes in the seventeenth or eighteenth century, sometimes in England, sometimes on the Continent.

What journeys you described, what sieges of castles and cities! Then there were the knights who rode through plain and forest, the ladies who were defended and freed and protected by them, the stout craftsmen and fine humble characters you contrasted with the nobles, to show them up. Oh, what astonishing, wonderful things you mixed with the ordinary and the familiar, with dwarfs and astrologers, wizards, witches and gipsies! What spells and sorceries, mysterious messages and horoscopes, what complicated plots and unexpected solutions!

And all of them spotless: books that exalt goodness and loyalty and can be put into the hands of children. When I compare them with the present flood of evil from the presses I say with amazement: all honour to this Scotsman, father of the fine historical novel!

* * *

Recently I re-read your *Anne of Geierstein*, and this is what I found in it. The hero, a brave young man called Arthur, is riding to the court of Provence with Thiebault, a descendant of the troubadours, who loves ballads and sings with great charm and skill to his companion on the way. He sings of a troubadour, William Cabestainy, who loved Margaret, the wife of a baron called Raymond de Roussillon. The husband discovered their meetings, killed Cabestainy, cut out his heart, had it prepared like that of an animal, and served it to his wife. When she had

151

eaten this horrible meal, he told her what it consisted of. 'The lady replied, that since she had been made to partake of food so precious, no coarser morsel should ever after cross her lips. She persisted in her resolution, and thus starved herself to death. The troubadour, who celebrated this tragic history, had displayed in his composition a good deal of poetic art. Glossing over the error of the lovers as the fault of their destiny, dwelling on their tragic fate with considerable pathos, and finally execrating the blind fury of the husband with the full fervour of poetic indignation, he recorded, with vindictive pleasure, how every bold knight and true lover in the South of France assembled to besiege the baron's castle, stormed it by main force, left not one stone upon another, and put the tyrant himself to an ignominious death.'

Arthur, having listened to the story, says severely: 'Thiebault, sing me no more such lays. I have heard my father say, that the readiest mode to corrupt a Christian man, is to bestow upon vice the pity and praise which are due only to virtue. Your Baron of Roussillon is a monster of cruelty, but your unfortunate lovers were not the less guilty. It is by giving fair names to foul actions, that those who would start at real vice are led to practice its lessons, under the disguise of virtue.'

'I would you knew, Seignor,' answers Thiebault, 'that this lay of Cabestainy and the Lady Margaret of Roussillon is reckoned a masterpiece of the joyous science. Fie, sir, you are too young to be so strict a censor of morals. What will you do when your head is grey, if you are thus severe when it is scarcely brown?'

'A head which listens to folly in youth will hardly be honourable in old age,' Arthur retorts.

One of the Fathers of the Church might have spoken like that. But you, Sir Walter, were more effective than the Fathers would have been. First of all, because the Fathers were preachers, and as a rule preachers are thought to be against their audience—though this may not be so. Whereas you, by offering your readers enjoyment and escape, seem to be in favour of them, on their side. Secondly, because you were clever enough to give the hero, who is unconditionally loved by the reader, moral lessons to propound. It's Horace's old trick—mixing what is useful with what is enjoyable.

* * *

Today, alas, the trick used by you and Horace is no longer employed very often. In the newspapers and comics read by our children, and in the weekly magazines, the hero may hand out punches when he has to, but he seldom helps the weak and the oppressed, as your heroes did. More often it's the evil hero who comes out on top and is given victory in the end.

It is certainly hard to find charming, cheerful, feeling heroines in fiction, girls who are modest and reserved as well, whose knights tremblingly lay all they have and all they are at their feet. Your heroines, Sir Walter, have sensitive feelings and often blush. Today's fictional girls never blush; they smoke and drink and giggle, they are shown either as biological entities or else as toys. Marriage isn't the usual ending of a novel. Very often girls in fiction aren't just corrupt but cynical and violent. In a detective story the girl's lover has punched her father; he lies on the ground, his face covered in blood. 'Do it again, hit him again!' she urges the boy. Another girl says: 'There's no fun in robbing the rich, so you've got to steal from the poor.'

You may ask me: but why do people write such things? I wonder myself, and I don't know the answer. Can it be that they're trying to protest, with these paradoxically immoral ideas, against a society they think is hypocritical in its moral outlook? The trouble is that the young don't understand irony and caricature. Instead, they gradually absorb the evil and are morally poisoned.

Maybe they want their reading to provide an exciting escape from the greyness and monotony of everyday life. But that's a mistake. Such reading becomes a drug that urges them to want stronger and stronger excitement, easier pleasures and rewards, which make them dislike hard work and academic studies.

Maybe the publishers want to make money by playing on the weakness of the young and on our baser instincts. I'm afraid this is it, more than anything. How stupid it is, then, to let ourselves be used by such money-grubbers. The preacher said: 'You are more stupid than mice.' Mice fall into traps, but at least they aren't paying for the privilege of doing so. You fall into traps when we read such things, and actually pay the men who laid them for us.

Sir Walter, in *Waverley*, your first novel, there is the following passage: 'A weekly post brought, in those days, to Waverley-Honour, a *Weekly Intelligencer*, which, after it had satisfied Sir Everard's curiosity, his sister's, and that of his aged butler, was regularly transferred from the Hall to the Rectory, from the Rectory to Squire Stubbs' at the Grange, from the Squire to the Baronet's steward at his neat white house on the heath, from the steward to the bailiff, and from him through a huge circle of honest dames and gaffers, by whose hard and horny hands it was generally worn to pieces in about a month after its arrival.'

I wish you could see things today! Vast quantities of newspaper roll off the presses every morning, are loaded onto trains and vans and delivered to the news-stands and kiosks. On the buses, as they go to work, people sitting or standing have their newspapers unfolded, and are reading so avidly that they often have no idea of what is going on around them. Office workers pass round an interesting article, discuss it, tell jokes the moment they have read them. People in restaurants have a plate a little to their right, a newspaper beside it, on the left. Children read newspapers at school and pass them secretly round in lessons— not always the cleanest of papers, either.

The other day, when I got off the train in Rome, I noticed railway workers picking up newspapers left on the seats, and taking them away, pleased with the thought of reading them later, comfortably at home. People love the press, and soon newspapers will come into their homes projected on a kind of television screen and we shall be able to choose what we want and sit there reading it. Add the radio and television to all this and you'll see what an enormous problem faces parents, teachers, pastors of souls and public authorities.

The problem is all the greater because people guard their

freedom jealously, and censorship and prohibitions are impossible to impose today. Will the state find a way of limiting freedom when it is clearly against the public good? Will the young accept hints and signals, at least? Motorists aren't the least bit upset by the orders given by traffic lights. None of them protests that he's intelligent and mature, and knows and understands everything about himself. Why don't we humbly accept some moral traffic lights, then?

One day, Sir Walter, you were a little worried. You and your wife were walking through a field full of sheep and pretty little lambs. 'How lovely they are!' you exclaimed. 'Yes,' said your wife, 'they're delicious, especially with mint sauce.' At that moment you failed entirely to understand each other.

*   *   *

All honour to the Scotsman! I say this sincerely but with a slight reservation about the small arrows you shot off occasionally at the Catholic Church. It was quite understandable—you were a Presbyterian, undoubtedly in good faith. But I was a boy in love with my Church, and it made me a little uneasy. The good you did remains, though; and your exemplary life. So, all praise and honour to you, Sir Walter! I wish Christians, and especially the young, would understand you and follow you into the calm waters of the spirit and imagination in which you loved to live, and to take your readers.

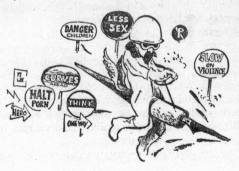

To the Unknown Painter at the Castle

Dear Unknown Painter,

I haven't been able to discover your name. But I liked your four paintings hanging in a corner room, lit by small Gothic windows in this old castle. Artistically they were modest enough, but their moral meaning made me pause and reflect, and seemed to me persuasive.

The first painting represents childhood. A sailing boat has just come into port. In it sits a child, gazing serenely at the waves. He can sit there calmly because an angel is holding the tiller firmly in the foreground. Behind, on the deck, is a dark figure, but it is in a profound sleep.

The second painting represents adolescence. The child of the first painting is now a young man. He stands in the boat, looking with curiosity into the unknown distance, where he imagines all kinds of wonderful things. The tiller is still in the angel's hands, but the waves are much bigger and the dark figure is no longer asleep: his grim eyes bode no good; they gaze longingly at the tiller, and suggest that an attack is on its way:

The third painting represents maturity. There is now a man in the boat, a man fighting with all his strength against a raging hurricane and a background of devils. The sky is dark; the man is dark; the tiller is in the hands of the dark figure; the angel has been relegated to the background.

In the fourth picture an old man sits in the boat. The storm has abated, the port is in sight, the sun gilds the waves. The angel is in charge of the boat and the dark figure is bound with strong chains.

* * *

Dear painter, I agree with you. Our life is a journey, with a departure and an arrival: our twenty, fifty or sixty years are merely a period between these two extremes.

But while we know exactly when we arrive, we are completely

156

ignorant of when we are leaving. How many years have we still? There are plenty of clever people, who know about drawing and mechanics, English and trigonometry; but this tiny fact, this insignificant detail of the years remaining, nobody knows. A shiver runs through the mind, seeming to suggest this: 'I may have very little time left, perhaps only a month or a few days. Lord, I won't waste a single moment.'

There is an even more worrying problem. There are two ports at which we may land, Heaven and Hell; only the first is desirable, and represents the climax of good fortune. Shall we get there? That's the problem. In comparison with this all other problems mean nothing. That a man is rich and famous and has had a splendid career means nothing if he doesn't get there. He's got to get to that final, blessed port!

* * *

To be good we must struggle, I agree, especially at certain times—that is, when it's hardest. Two opposing forces are fighting for the tiller of our life. Sanctity is the fruit of conquest, I agree, the result of victories gained each day with the sword.

This is all true. Paul wrote: 'For we wrestle not against flesh and blood, but against principalities, against powers, against the rulers of the darkness of this world, against spiritual wickedness in high places.' The Pope recently reminded us of this truth.

* * *

I agree with you, too, about our human passions. Dante describes them at the beginning of his journey, when he finds his way barred by three wild beasts: the panther, the lion and the wolf.

The panther, which is light and quick and gives no respite, is sensuality; it exploits everything that will put out the tastes and joys of the spirit in us and will arouse evil desires. We feel it snapping at our heels wherever we go and, without God's help and protection we might well feel depressed and discouraged.

The lion, with its head held high, is pride. This aims straight at the head, which is held high, even though the chest and stomach below it may be poking out awkwardly. This sort of pride is never justified. There was a President in Guiseppe Giusti's time who was very proud of his position. He wore a tall hat and during sittings laid it on an armchair. One day somebody sat on it by mistake and a poet wrote: 'They squashed the President's top hat: luckily, there was nothing inside.'

Oh, some people wear top hats even in the presence of God! They're everything, they know everything, they're stuck-up, non-conformist, self-sufficient, argumentative prigs! So what? What lies underneath it all? And what have they got to be so pleased about?

The wolf is lean all burning with desires. It represents worldliness, which devours us with its endless commitments: social life, exams, competitions, business, sport, entertainment. We allow ourselves to be sucked down by these things as if into an abyss.

And what about God? What about our souls? Such things become small and secondary; we glimpse them now and then like distant dots, to which we give a few moments on rare, fleeting occasions, suddenly and ridiculously turning our values upside down.

* * *

I agree with you that the forces of good mount counter-offensives, using very different tactics from those of the wild beasts. Just as well!

As far as sensuality is concerned, it isn't a bad idea to consider 'emptiness' as a protection. There are times when God creates a sense of emptiness within us. We feel that some things aren't worthy of us, aren't enough, don't satisfy us.

This year, 1973, is the centenary of the birth of Trilussa. He wrote: 'A bee lights on a rosebud; it sucks and goes away. All in all, happiness is a small thing.'

But very often it isn't even happiness we're talking about;

just transient pleasure. Often actually the opposite of pleasure, a kind of toothache; while a voice cries: 'Go to the dentist!'

St Augustine, referring to the seventeen years of his unruly life, confessed: 'I was gnawed, I tortured myself during those years; that wasn't a life, Lord!' St Camillus warned himself and others thus: 'When we do evil we feel pleasure, but the pleasure soon passes and the evil remains; doing good is difficult, but the difficulty soon passes and the good remains.'

To combat pride we need the Gospel, which is perfectly clear about it: 'Put yourself in the lowest place.' Our Lord was 'like one who serves' among his Apostles and said: 'You must wash each others feet . . . and are blessed if you do this.'

To fight worldliness, here's another small thought from the Gospel: 'What does it profit a man if he gains the whole world and loses his own soul? What can a man give in exchange for his soul?'

* * *

Dear friend, dear unknown painter, your paintings succeeded in touching some fibre of my soul. And in giving me pleasure.

But now I'm beginning to feel uneasy. 'Why's that?' you may say. Well, I'll tell you in confidence: I'm afraid that I may have upset my readers. Some of them will have found me romantic, ingenuous, an old fogey who goes round looking at castles. The moment they sniffed a hint of moralizing, they'll have stopped reading.

Ah, well, that's one of the snags I have to put up with.

HIPPOCRATES, a Greek doctor (? 460–? 370 BC), contemporary of
Socrates, who is known as the father of medicine. He insisted on the
autonomy of medical studies, freed from interference by philosophy,
and maintained that all illnesses have natural causes. He classified
man's temperament into four parts: impulsive, phlegmatic, irascible and
melancholy.

3

To Hippocrates

Dear Hippocrates,

You were a contemporary of Socrates and like him a philosopher; and you were a physician as well. It was in the field of medicine that you shone more than in that of philosophy. And for three main reasons.

Firstly, after wandering over most of the known world, observing and noting things very carefully, you wrote a number of books that stimulated medical science for centuries.

Secondly, you set down the famous Hippocratic oath, a moral code of unequalled value. Using it, doctors swear to prescribe what their patients need and to protect them from everything unjust and harmful; not to end a pregnancy; to have only one aim when they enter a house—the cure of the sick—and to refrain from corrupting anyone, man or woman, even slaves; and to keep professional secrecy as a sacred trust.

Thirdly, you were the first to classify the four fundamental temperaments of man: impulsive, phlegmatic, irascible, and melancholy. I know that Nicola Pende and others after you tried to suggest new classifications, which were more scientific but more complicated as well, Your temperate, correct classification has lasted now for more than twenty-five centuries.

* * *

Let's put these four temperaments to the test, and let the test be a wall of rock that is to be climbed.

First comes the *impulsive* man.

He glances up at the wall and says: 'Oh, that's nothing. I'll get up it quickly.' At once he attacks it with ardour and enthusiasm. But he hasn't foreseen anything, or provided himself with the most elementary tools. Large difficulties soon loom up, in the face of which our impetuous climber realizes that keenness and muscular strength aren't enough.

Then, from great enthusiasm, he goes to the opposite extreme.

'I'm giving up—this rock's hopeless.'

In this, he's like Tartarin of Tarascon, of whom Daudet writes: 'Don Quixote and Sancho Panza in the one same man! . . . two Tartarins—Quixote-Tartarin and Sancho-Tartarin! Quixote-Tartarin firing up . . . and shouting: "Up and at 'em!" and Sancho-Tartarin thinking only of the rheumatics ahead, and murmuring "I mean to stay at home"

THE DUET

QUIXOTE-TARTARIN (*Highly excited*)	SANCHO-TARTARIN (*Quite calmly*)
Cover yourself with glory, Tartarin	Tartarin, cover yourself with flannel.
(*Still more excitedly*)	(*Still more calmly*)
O for the terrible double-barrelled rifle! O for bowie knives, lassoes and moccasins!	O for the thick knitted waistcoats! and warm knee caps! O for the welcome padded caps with ear-flaps!
(*Above all self-control*)	(*Ringing up the maid*)
A battleaxe! fetch me a battleaxe!	Now then, Jeannette, do bring up that chocolate!

Whereupon Jeannette would appear with an unusually good cup of chocolate, just right for warmth, sweetly smelling . . . which would set Sancho-Tartarin off on the broad grin, and into a laugh that drowned the shouts of Quixote-Tartarin.'

This is what the impulsive man is like: easily filled with enthusiasm, but inconstant; an optimist in the case of something that concerns himself and his own capacity, but unthinking, relying too much on feeling and imagination. He has good in him, but if he wants to achieve more in his life he must get used to reflecting, to making detailed, well-considered plans, to following the advice of the bishop who said to a new parish priest: 'Go ahead. First of all, see; then foresee; and finally, proceed.'

* * *

Next the *phlegmatic* man comes to the wall.

He looks up at it once, twice, many times; and makes his calculations: 'Here we must plan to climb on pitons, then come down on a rope, then climb up on ice.'

He consults maps, takes notes, makes lists of the things he needs and gets hold of them: thick rope, thin rope, ice axe, pitons for rock and for ice, a wooden wedge and a hammer, a rucksack and hobnailed boots. The whole thing is carried out without either time-wasting or hurry, and while he gets ready the phlegmatic man chews gum and says: 'Maybe I'll do it.' Well, in spite of all obstacles, he does. This was the style of General de Gaulle, who from childhood was icy cold; so much so that his brothers used to say of him: 'Charles must have fallen into a bowl of ice!'

During a battle a lieutenant who brought a message was looking for General de Gaulle and unable to find him. 'Go out into the field,' a driver told him. 'You'll find him there. And if you don't, look on the ground and you'll find him by following the track of his cigarette stubs.' The lieutenant did this and arrived to find the General sitting calmly under a tree, smoking like a chimney. Having read the message, de Gaulle gave orders to the officers standing by him and, without losing his calm, carried on smoking, merely saying: 'You'll see, things will get better.' Which is what happened.

The phlegmatic is a fortunate temperament in one way. In another, it may produce apathetic, insensitive people who are neither very sociable nor very communicative. A little more enthusiasm, a greater, more obvious interest in other people's business, would make them more amiable and sympathetic.

* * *

Now here is the *choleric-irascible* man.

'Obstacles on this wall?' he bursts out. 'Why, obstacles are there to be overcome!' and he attacks it furiously, seeing it as an enemy. He doesn't spare himself, uses all his energy, all his competitiveness; often achieving brilliant results on the way but not always reaching the top.

The choleric man has a deep, lively sensitivity; he is quick to take decisions, tenacious in carrying them out, but needs to be more affectionate and calm, and has to protect himself against both enthusiasm and excessive pessimism. The Abyssinian Ras Tafari would say to him: 'Yes, you've got two legs, but you can climb only one tree at a time!' If you listened to him, though, you'd say he could climb a whole forest at once!

There's also, apart from the good in him, a fair amount of useless stuff he must free himself from. In trying to eliminate obstacles he may create others, and make a remarkable number of enemies. Unless, like the scold Zantippe, he has the luck to meet only people with the patience of Socrates.

Socrates, Zantippe's husband, used to say: 'I married her deliberately, cross-grained as she is, because once I could bear her I was sure I could bear anyone else.' Once, to avoid listening to her complaints, he sat down in the doorway of the house. Zantippe, in a fury, went to the window and flung a bucket of water over him. 'I might have known,' said the placid Socrates, 'after the thunder came the rain.'

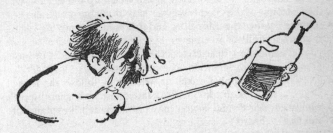

The *melancholy* man, in contrast to the angry one, is depressed and undervalues himself. 'Don't you see it's impossible to climb a wall like this? D'you want me to kill myself?' he asks. From the start he lets himself be scared off by difficulties; he's a born pessimist. When he sees a bottle of wine he grumbles: 'This is the very first time in my life that I've wanted a drink, and I find a bottle that's half empty. What terrible bad luck!' What he ought to say is: 'Why, there's still half a bottle to drink! Who'd have thought it! What fantastic luck!'

The strength to see the good side of things should be characteristic of the Christian. If the Gospel really means 'good news', then being a Christian means being a happy man, one who spreads joy. 'Gloomy faces,' said St Philip Neri, 'aren't made for the happy house of Paradise.'

You see, Hippocrates, how I have moved on from your classifications into Paradise. Down here we must strive to get up there, accepting the temperament handed on to us by our parents, although improving on it and, by our own efforts, trying to produce a fine character out of it.

Up there is St Thomas Aquinas, a saint so phlegmatic that if an ox had walked into his room he'd have carried on studying. And St Jean Eudes, who boiled with rage if he so much as saw a heretic. Francis de Sales, the saint of good manners, an artist in speech and letters, is there with the Curé of Ars, who was a champion at whipping his own back and ate potatoes that had gone mouldy after being cooked a week before.

St Peter, the great porter who will weigh up our deserts, will take account of the good works we have done but must also put into the balance the difficulties and delays and stumbling-blocks that are a result of our uneven temperament. Whether he uses your classification, dear Hippocrates, or that of Pende, or bases himself on the scientific characterization of Spranger or Kretschmer, Jung or Kunkel, or whether he follows the tests of Don Cojazzi, I don't know. This latter test isn't scientific; it's wholly empirical; and as you may not know it I'll explain it to you as I've heard Cojazzi explain it.

Well, Cojazzi says that the best place to discover people's temperaments is in a cheap restaurant. Or, to be exact, in a cheap restaurant where a thirsty man who has ordered a glass of beer has it brought to him with a big fly struggling in it.

Is the customer an Englishman? Phlegmatically he puts the glass down on the table; calmly he rings the bell and calmly orders: 'Another glass of beer, cool and clean, please.' Having drunk it he pays and goes out, neither moved nor upset. If anyone is upset it is the waiter, not because of the fly but because of the tip he didn't get.

Is the glass of beer served to a Frenchman? He sees the fly and goes berserk. He slams down the glass, swears and shouts at the owner and the waiters, goes out slamming the door and in the street carries on ranting against the restaurant, the beer and the fly.

An Italian comes in, looks at the fly, and smilingly flicks his middle finger at it to chase it off the surface of the beer. He jokes with the waiter: 'Look, I asked you for a drink and you've brought me something to eat,' but he drinks it all the same and leaves, forgetting to pay the bill.

Now it's the turn of a German: he sees the fly, keeps the glass raised to the height of his nose and frowns, shuts his eyes, puts back his head a little, and, being highly disciplined, sends down both beer and fly in a single gulp.

A Dane comes in. He is much amused to see the fly in the foam of the beer and takes out his glasses. So wholly taken up is he with the sight that he would forget to drink if the waiter, having noticed the fly, didn't change the first glass of beer for a second, with effusive apologies.

Last of all is the Eskimo. He's never seen a fly and thinks that the one before him is a favourite local dish, a speciality. So he eats the fly and throws away the beer.

Now forgive me, illustrious Hippocrates. It may seem like profanation to set these trifles beside your serious scientific ideas. But suppose it works? Does it show that even ordinary people's good sense seizes upon the absurd and castigates it, and that there is such a thing as a primitive temperament, uncontrolled and unimproved?

St Theresa of the Child Jesus (Thérèse de Lisieux 1873–97) had no
notable outward events in her life, but a rich inner life of dedication
and love. She entered the Carmelite convent at Lisieux and died at
an early age of consumption. She wrote a much-read spiritual autobiography, *The Story of a Soul*, which has been translated into thirty
languages.

To St Theresa of Lisieux

Dear little Theresa,

I was seventeen when I read your autobiography.

It struck me forcibly. You called it 'The story of a spring flower'. To me the will-power, courage and decisiveness it showed made it seem more like the story of a piece of steel. Once you had chosen the path of complete dedication to God, nothing could stop you: not illness, nor opposition from outside, nor inner confusion and darkness.

I remember the time I was ill and sent to a sanatorium, in the days before penicillin and antibiotics, when death awaited pretty well anyone who was sent to hospital.

I was ashamed of myself for feeling a little afraid. 'At the age of twenty-three,' I said to myself, 'Theresa, who until then had been healthy and full of vitality, was filled with joy and hope when she first spat blood. Not only that, but when her health improved, she got permission to end her fast with a diet of dry bread and water. And you're almost trembling! You're a priest! Stir yourself! Don't be silly!'

* * *

Reading it again, when we have come to the centenary of your birth (1873 to 1973), what now strikes me most is the way in which you loved God and your neighbour. St Augustine wrote: 'We reach God, not by walking, but through love.' You also called your road 'the way of love'. Christ said: 'No one comes to me unless my Father calls him'. You were perfectly in tune with these words, feeling 'like a bird without strength and without wings', and seeing in God an eagle who came down to carry you off on high, on its wings. You called divine grace 'the lifter', which carried you to God swiftly and easily, since you were 'too small to climb the harsh ladder of perfection'.

I said 'easily'. But let me make it clear: I meant it only in one way. In another . . . well, in the final months of your life your soul felt as if it was going down a kind of dark passage, seeing nothing of what it had once seen clearly. 'Faith,' you wrote, 'is no longer a veil but a wall.' Your physical sufferings were so great that you said: 'If I had not had faith, I would have chosen death.' In spite of that, you kept saying to the Lord you loved, saying with your will alone: 'I sing of the happiness of Paradise, but without any feeling of joy; I sing simply because I *want to believe*.' Your last words were: 'My God, I love you.'

To the merciful love of God you offered yourself as a victim. All this did not prevent you from enjoying what was good and beautiful. Before your final illness you loved painting, and wrote poetry and short plays on religious subjects, taking some of the parts yourself and showing quite a talent for acting. In the last stage of your illness, when you felt briefly better, you asked for some chocolates. You had no fear of your own imperfections, not even of having sometimes slept during meditation, out of weariness ('mothers love their children, even when they are asleep').

Loving your neighbour, you tried to serve others in small, useful ways, but to do so unobserved; and you preferred, if anything, to do this for people who irritated you, those you understood least. Behind their unlikeable faces you sought the beloved face of Christ. And no one noticed these efforts of yours. 'How mystical she was in chapel, and at her work', the prioress wrote of you. 'At other times she was very amusing, full of fun and making us all laugh uproariously at recreation.'

The few lines certainly don't contain the whole of your message to Christians. But they are enough to point a few things out to us.

* * *

True love of God is linked with a definite decision; this has to be taken and, when need be, renewed. The indecisive Metastasio, who said: 'Confused—and sadly doubting—I go not, nor do I remain', is not the kind of person who really loves God.

Your fellow countryman, Marshal Foch, was nearer to it. During the Battle of the Marne he telegraphed: 'The main body of our army is giving way, the left is in retreat, but I am attacking just the same.' A touch of competiveness, a liking for risks, in no way compromises our love for God. You had it, dear Theresa, and with good reason felt that Joan of Arc was a sister-in-arms.

*   *   *

In Donizzetti's *l'Elisir d'amore* the 'secret tears' Adina weeps are enough to make her lover Nemorino feel reassured and happy. God does not want merely secret tears. He likes external tears so long as they match a decision we have made, a decision of the will. It is the same with outward good works: they please him only if they correspond to an inner love. Religious fasting had actually made the Pharisees' faces thin, but these thin faces did not appeal to Christ because the Pharisees' hearts were a long way from God. You, dear Theresa, wrote: 'Love should lie not in feeling, but in works.' Yet you added: 'God does not need our works, only our love.' Perfect!

*   *   *

We may love all kinds of other fine things, so long as nothing we love is against, or above, or in the same measure as God. In other words the love of God should not be exclusive, it should suffuse the rest of life.

Jacob fell in love with Rachel, and in order to win her served for seven long years; which, said the Bible, 'seemed to him but a few days, for the love he had to her.' And God had nothing against this, in fact he approved of it and blessed it.

But to sprinkle with holy water and bless all the affections of this world is quite another matter. Unfortunately, this is just what some churchmen are trying to do today, under the influence of the ideas of Freud, Kinsey and Marcuse; they praise what is known as the new sexual morality. If they want to avoid confusion and mushy attitudes, Christians should look not to these churchmen but to the teaching of the Church, which gives them special help both in preserving the doctrine of Christ unspoiled, and in adapting it to our own time in the right way.

* * *

Seeking the face of Christ in the face of our neighbour is the only way of making sure that we really love everyone, overcoming dislikes and ideologies, and mere philanthropical feelings.

A young man—old Archbishop Perini wrote—knocks at a front door. He is wearing his best suit and has a flower in his buttonhole, but his heart is beating fast. Will the girl and her family welcome the proposal of marriage he has come so shyly to make?

The girl opens the door herself. He glances at her; her blush, her obvious pleasure (no 'secret tears'!) reassure him, and his heart swells. He goes in and sees the girl's mother, who seems to him so extraordinarily nice that he would like to hug her. Then there's her father, whom he's met a hundred times, but who this evening seems transfigured by some special light. Later the girl's two brothers turn up and there are slaps on the back and warm greetings.

What is happening to this young man, Perini wonders. What are all these affections that have suddenly sprouted like mushrooms? The answer is that it isn't a matter of many affections but of a single one: he loves the girl, and the love he feels for her spreads over all her relations. Anyone who seriously loves Christ cannot refuse to love men, who are Christ's brothers. Love should transform a little even those who are ugly, evil and dull.

* * *

Love modestly. Often this is the only thing possible. I've never had a chance of diving into a roaring stream to save someone in danger; but I'm often asked to lend something, to write letters, to give a bit of easy advice. I've never met a dog with hydrophobia, but I've known plenty of maddening flies and mosquitoes. I've never been beaten by persecutors, but plenty of people have disturbed me shouting in the road, having their television sets on too loud, or even making slurping noises as they ate their soup.

Helping where we can, not getting worked up, being understanding, remaining calm and smiling at these times (as far as possible!) means loving our neighbour without big words, but in a practical way. Christ practised this sort of charity a great deal. What patience he had in putting up with the way the Apostles quarrelled among themselves! And how careful he was to encourage and to praise. 'I have not found such faith in Israel,' he said of the Centurion and of the Canaan woman. 'You stayed with me even in difficult times,' he told the Apostles. And once he asked Peter if he would lend him his boat.

'Lord of all courtesy,' Dante calls him. He knew how to put himself in others' shoes, and how to suffer with them. He protected and defended others, as well as forgiving sinners: Zacheus, the woman taken in adultery, Magdalene. You, in Lisieux, followed his example, and we should do as much out in the world.

Carnegie told a story about a woman who laid the table for her husband and sons, with flowers on it, but on each plate put a handful of hay. 'What's this? Hay to eat?' they cried: 'Oh no, I'm bringing the meal on soon,' she said. 'But let me just say one thing: for years I've cooked for you, tried to vary the food—rice one day, soup the next, a joint, a casserole and so on. But you never say you like it, you never praise my cooking. For heaven's sake say something! I'm not a stone and I can't carry on without recognition or encouragement!'

Charity in social or public matters may be quite modest too. Suppose there's a justified strike: this may bring trouble to all sorts of people not directly involved in the dispute. Accepting discomfort, not grumbling, feeling solidarity with our brothers who are fighting in defence of their rights, is pure Christian charity. Not much noticed, but none the worse for that.

Joy mixed with Christian love appears in the song of the angels at Bethlehem. It is part of the essence of the Gospel, which means 'good news'. It is characteristic of the great saints. 'A sad saint,' St Theresa of Avila used to say, 'is a poor saint.' 'Among us here,' said St Dominic Savio, 'we make saints merrily!' Joy may become perfect charity if it is shared, as in fact, dear St Theresa, you shared yours at recreation in the convent.

There is a story of an Irishman who died suddenly and went up for divine judgement, feeling extremely uneasy. He didn't think he had done much good on earth! There was a queue ahead of him, so he settled down to look and listen. After consulting his big book, Christ said to the first man in the queue: 'I see here that I was hungry and you gave me to eat. Good man! Go on into Heaven.' To the second he said: 'I was thirsty and you gave me to drink,' and to the third: 'I was in prison and you visited me.' And so it went on.

As each man ahead of him was sent to Heaven the Irishman examined his conscience and felt he had a great deal to fear. He'd never given anyone food or drink, he hadn't visited prisoners or the sick. Then his turn came. Trembling he watched Christ examining the book. Then Christ looked up and said: 'Well, there's not much written here, but you did do something: I was sad and discouraged and depressed; you came and told me funny stories, made me laugh and cheered me up. Get along to Heaven!'

That's a joke, of course, but it makes the point that no form of charity should be neglected or undervalued.

*   *   *

Theresa, the love you gave God (and your neighbour for love of God) was really worthy of him. This is how our love should be: a flame fed by all that's great and fine in ourselves; a rejection of all that's refractory in us; and a victory that carries us on its wings and takes us as a gift to the feet of God.

ALESSANDRO MANZONI (1785–1873) was a celebrated Italian author and convinced Catholic. He wrote the greatest Italian novel, *The Betrothed* (*I Promessi Sposi*), plays and religious poetry. He was an aristocrat by birth, but believed that the only true aristocracy were those who served the poor.

To Alessandro Manzoni

Dear Don Lisander,

When you died, a century ago, your friends in the humble room with you all said: 'A new saint has gone up to heaven today.'

Later the candid, generous Antonio Cojazzi fought for the cause of your canonisation to be officially taken up by the Church. All these people exaggerated a little.

On the other hand, Maria Luisa Astaldi and others also exaggerated recently, when, in a cheap, novelettish way, they showed you as a man suffering from a hereditary illness, an incurable neurotic tormented by terrible doubts about your faith.

The truth is quite different. Some complexes resulting from your temperament and from an unhappy domestic situation did affect you, but you were nonetheless a great Catholic, sincere and convinced. Even as an old man you went to communion every day.

What your life was like can be seen from the holy thoughts that fill your writings. This, for instance: 'Life is not meant to be a burden to many and a feast for a few, but a commitment which everyone must take on'; 'unhappiness is not suffering and being poor; it is doing wrong'; 'the very thought of arousing dissension makes me sad'; 'God never ruffles the joy of his children, except to prepare them for a certain, far greater joy'.

Whatever your pen touched, gleams of religious faith came out of it. This could not have happened if the mind and heart that directed your hand to write had not been full of religion. *The Betrothed* bears witness to this feeling from beginning to end. It isn't surprising, in fact, that Ludovico da Casoria, a monk and a holy man, could say of it—a novel and a love story—that 'it could be read in a choir of virgins, presided over by the Madonna'.

* * *

Your novel is a story of poor people. The places in which it mainly takes place are poor: the mountain, the countryside, the lake. The main characters are poor: Renzo and Lucia, good young people who want to love each other. Renzo has prepared a place for his beloved, who often looks at it, with a quick blush, as she passes, thinking with pleasure of the happy time when she will be there permanently. But a storm breaks and the pair are parted. 'It's for the Lord to provide,' Lucia says at the worst moment. 'Whatever God wills,' says Renzo, though he never gives up trying, boldly and manfully.

Around them are people just as simple and honest. Agnese, Lucia's mother, illiterate but practical, who gives them decisive advice. 'Wit and courage and it's easy,' she tells Renzo and Lucia, when planning their surprise-marriage. '. . . and the marriage is all done, and as binding as if the Pope himself had tied them up.'

There are many others besides Agnese: a hesitant, selfish, timid priest, Don Abbondio, who is anxious to save his own skin, more than anything; Perpetua, his housekeeper, who gives him good advice; Ambrogio, the sacristan; a very practical inn-keeper; 'Paolin dei Morti', the grave-digger; Tonio, with his simple-minded brother Gervasio and a wife to whom he's lied a great deal; Bettina, the little girl who cries joyfully: 'The bridegroom, the bridegroom!'; Menico, the boy who's very good at stone-skimming.

And who is this turning up at the door of the house saying 'Deo gratias'? It is Fra Galdino, looking for walnuts, his satchel dangling from his left shoulder, who tells of a great miracle that has taken place in the monastery of Romagna. And what about this monk who comes to Agnese's door and stands on the threshold? It is a saintly man, Fra Cristofero, the spiritual father of Lucia, whose conscience he has tempered, making a pure, strong woman, full of faith and hope, out of a poor peasant girl, alone in the world with her mother.

*　　*　　*

All these live in the village. Within the village, and outside it too, you created as many as two hundred and fifty-five characters, dear Don Lisander; all of them brought alive, if only in a few words—like the fat man who stands stiffly in his shop doorway, looking as if he would prefer to ask questions rather than to answer them; like Don Gonzalo's trumpeter; or like Ferrer's coachman, who in the midst of the crowd and tumult smiles 'with ineffable politeness' and says: 'Please, gentlemen, a little room, a very little—just enough to let us pass.'

But what about the great ones of this world? In your novel you bring some of them in. Some of them serve the poor, but some of them are shown up by the poor and humble. You were an aristocrat by birth but you believed there was only one aristocracy, and that was found in serving the poor, 'No man is superior to any other except in serving others,' you wrote.

Cardinal Federigo, Fra Cristofero, the Unnamed, who is converted, the Marquis, heir to Don Rodrigo, the comfortably-off merchant's widow—all these belong to the aristocracy of souls, because they help the poor. The other aristocratic characters, especially those who are violent and bullying, you don't like at all, as you make perfectly clear. There is a prince who 'destined all the younger children of either sex to the cloister, so as to leave the family fortune for the eldest son, whose function it was to perpetuate the family, to have children and so to torture himself by tormenting them in the same way'. Don Rodrigo is a powerful man who doesn't fear God; he fears the world, though, and despises the humble folk among whom he lives. He is capable of insulting a poor friar and throwing him out of the house, but he is terrified of the Order he belongs to ('Do you expect me to bring all the Capuchins of Italy down on me?').

Of the prince who forces his daughter to become a nun, you say 'We have not the heart to call him at this moment by the name of father'. You condemn without indulgence Don Rodrigo's hard-working, hypocritical uncle in the Secret Council ('ambiguous language, significant silences, sudden pauses in the middle of a sentence, winks that mean "my lips are sealed", raising hopes without committing himself, conveying a threat amidst elaborate

179

politeness . . .'). You condemn Count Attilio, a great supporter of beatings ('a stick doesn't soil anyone's hands') and Dr Azzecca-garbugli [Quibble-weaver], a calculating opportunist, or rather a charlatan and a puppet in the hands of the powerful whom he supports in their oppression of the poor.

* * *

You dislike violence at all times, even when the poor are unjustly oppressed and seek to use it. Renzo decides to take justice into his own hands ('I'll carry out my own justice, I will!'), and you crush him with the harsh comment that a man overwhelmed with grief cannot tell what he is saying. And what do you advise in place of violence? Forgiveness. Fra Cristofero asks pardon of the brother of a man he has killed, and for the rest of his life preaches forgiveness. In his satchel he carries the 'bread of forgiveness' and before he dies gives it to Renzo and Lucia with the words: 'Keep it: show it to your children . . . Tell them always to forgive; always. Everything, everything!'

To an angry, bewildered Renzo, he says: 'I also have hated . . . I killed a man I hated deeply, whom I had hated for a long time . . . D'you think that if there had been a good reason for it I would not have found it out in thirty years? Ah! If only I could instill into your heart the feeling I have always had, and still have, for the man I hated.'

The lesson is not in vain. Renzo forgives Don Rodrigo. But his pardon is mixed with renewed anger and becomes a wish for vengeance again in the flight from Monza to Milan, during which he 'killed Don Rodrigo in his heart and brought him to life again at least twenty times'. After further reproaches from Fra Cristofero at the *lazzaretto*, it becomes a heartfelt pardon once again; this pardon is repeated in Lucia's hut and once again at Don Rodrigo's death. 'From the heart, from the heart,' Fra Cristofero urges him to feel it.

* * *

Another feeling, linked with this one of non-violence, pervades the whole of your novel: this is, faith in Providence.

When Lucia says goodbye to the mountains she has lived among, she weeps in the boat but her last thought is: 'He who gave you so much happiness is everywhere'. Reluctant to agree to the surprise-wedding, she says: 'I want to be your wife, but by straightforward, God-fearing means, and before the altar. Let us leave it to Him above. Don't you think he can find a way out and help us better than we can ourselves by all this deception?'

Of Renzo in the wood, you say: 'Before stretching himself out on this bed which Providence had provided for him, he knelt to thank God for this blessing and for all the help which he had had from Him during that terrible day.' When his eyes close, his mind is full of whirling thoughts, but this one dominates the rest: 'God's will be done! He knows what he is doing; it's for our own good. May it all go to expiate my sins! Lucia is so good. God will not let her suffer for long, for long, for long . . .'

Renzo always keeps this attitude of trust in Providence. He remembers Providence before giving his few remaining coins to the poor at the gates of Bergamo. 'I said trust in Providence!' he exclaims when his cousin Bortolo helps him. 'I'll have to thank the Lord and the Madonna as long as I live,' he tells his friend, on his return from the *lazzaretto*.

'Finally,' you write, 'after discussing the question and casting around together a long time for a solution [Renzo and Lucia] came to the conclusion that . . . when [troubles] come, whether by our own fault or not, confidence in God can lighten them and turn them to our own improvement.'

Dear Don Lisander, all true followers of the Gospel will agree with that.

CASELLA, friend of Dante, possibly from Pistoia, a fine composer and musician. He set some of Dante's sonnets and songs to music, among them '*Amor che nella mente mi ragiona*'. Little is known of his life and death. In his *Divina Commedia* Dante meets him in the Ante Purgatorium while he is waiting to be carried across to Purgatory.

To Casella, musician

Dear musician and friend of Dante,

What you told Dante on the Mount of Purgatory is about to take place again. When he saw you arriving on the beach of the Ante Purgatorium at Easter in 1300, Dante was very much surprised. You had been dead for some time, and he could not understand why you had not yet been allowed into Purgatory, where you had been assigned to go.

You explained what had happened, and how the souls which were to go to Purgatory were gathered at a kind of pre-purgatorial station at Ostia, at the mouth of the Tiber. There an angel picked them up in his boat, but you had not been lucky enough to be chosen. Then, three months earlier, Pope Boniface VIII had proclaimed a Jubilee, and the angel had taken all those who wished to go. It was a time of mercy and forgiveness from which you were reaping advantages. And that was why you were there.

*　　*　　*

Today, instead of Pope Boniface, we have Pope Paul.

He too has proclaimed a Jubilee, dear Casella, although in rather different circumstances from those of 1300. Your Pope Boniface has a pretty uncertain tradition behind him. He had heard of other Jubilees in the past, but the investigation he set in motion turned up very little about them.

An old man from Savoy, aged a hundred and seven, said that, when he was a boy of seven in 1200, he had been to Rome with his father, who had made him promise to return there and benefit from the remarkable indulgences if he were still alive a

182

hundred years later. Two other old men from Beauvais said that a plenary indulgence had been granted a century before.

Tradition or no tradition, Pope Boniface did what many people had asked him to do and signed the Bull. There was a famous Jubilee: the whole of Europe seemed to come to Rome in the year 1300. People crowded in on foot and on horseback, pulling their old and sick along in carts. The basilicas of SS Peter and Paul stayed open night and day. The cardinals made the thirty visits prescribed for the Romans of Rome early in the morning; girls, who in those days were always confined to the house, made their visits at night, reliably chaperoned.

Among the famous pilgrims, dear Casella, were your Tuscan fellow-countrymen Dante, Giotto, and Giovanni Villani. From the pilgrimage Villani drew inspiration to write his history of Florence, as he tells us himself, and went home with his imagination fired by the sights he had seen in Rome. 'It was,' he writes, 'the most wonderful thing that was ever seen, that throughout the whole year there were in Rome, apart from the Romans themselves, two hundred thousand pilgrims, not counting those who came and went on the roads; and all of them were well looked after with food, horses as well as people, very patiently and without tumult or quarrels. To this I can bear witness because I was there and saw it. And much treasure came to the Church from the gifts of the pilgrims and the Romans became rich through selling their provisions' (Chronicle VIII, 36).

Unlike Boniface VIII, Paul VI has a Jubilee tradition behind him. The time established by Boniface and fixed by the saying: 'In Rome the hundredth year is always a Jubilee' was soon changed. A Jubilee took place every fifty years, then every twenty-five, so that anyone who wished to do so could profit by this great grace at least once in his lifetime.

And gradually, as the centuries passed, things progressed: better transport, a greater number of pilgrims. Trains, cars and aeroplanes brought many more than the two hundred thousand pilgrims of 1300 to Rome. Yet even in the Jubilee year of 1950 at least ten thousand individual pilgrims came to Rome on foot, on bicycles, on horseback, in canoes, in wheelchairs, pulled by dogs, or on wheeled stretchers.

Silvio Negro mentions the young Kurt Herming Drake, a Finnish student who left Helsinki in July and arrived in Rome in November. Baron Fritz von Gumpenberg, aged twenty-nine, who was almost blind, came on foot alone from his castle at Poltmes near Munich, and returned there on foot, once again going through Padua because of his devotion to St Anthony.

Pius XII gave a theme to this Jubilee: 'A great pardon and a great return.' Paul VI starts off the Jubilee with the word: 'Reconciliation.' Reconciliation between us and God, between us and our brothers, on the personal and on the social level. This is a wholly musical theme which you, Casella, if you were here, would sing sweetly as you sang to Dante, who retained a nostalgic memory of your song: 'Still its sweetness thrills me as of old,' he wrote.

* * *

Reconciliation with God, and the abandonment of the broad, winding road that leads to perdition: this is true music. Along this road gallop all the human passions riding on the horses of the Apocalypse: excessive desires, pride that is never satisfied with the pleasures, riches and honours it receives. Anyone who walks along that road will never be happy.

The great Tolstoy wrote of a horse who stopped on the way down a slope and refused to go on. 'I'm tired of pulling the carriage and obeying the coachman,' he said, 'So I'm stopping.' Of course he was perfectly free to do so but he paid dearly for it. From that moment everyone turned against him: the coachman who whipped him, the carriage that slipped down to crash into his legs, the passengers inside the carriage who shouted and cursed.

That's what happens. When we get on to the wrong road and turn against God, we overthrow order, break our pact of allegiance with God, give up his love, and rub ourselves up the wrong way, discontented with what we have done and eaten up with remorse.

Dear Casella, it's true that some people say songs are sung and sound very tuneful even on the wrong road. They reject Tolstoy's little story with contempt and declare that in sin they feel freer than ever. May I contradict them with just two words? These are 'master' and 'sickness'.

Whether we like it or not, sin becomes the sinner's master. At first it may flatter and caress him, but the sinner is still its slave and sooner or later he will feel the whip.

Now for 'sickness'. There are two kinds: unknown and obvious. A living, open wound hurts, but at least we know it exists and try to cure it. Think, on the other hand, of a hidden tumour: it grows and spreads, you don't know about it, delude yourself and your friends that you're well; then suddenly comes the change, the irreparable damage. That's what happens to someone full of sin who says he isn't and doesn't feel its weight. But imagine someone who carries a burden of sin but feels its weight on his back, and decides seriously to change his ways and to fling himself into the arms of Christ: what music that is, dear Casella.

* * *

Reconciliation between ourselves and our brothers is another sort of music. In your day there were fights between the Guelphs and the Ghibellines, between the Whites and the Blacks, between the Montecchi and the Cappelletti, the Montaldi and the Filippeschi and I don't know how many other factions. Your friend Dante wrote sadly and bitterly about these feuds.

Today, dear Casella, it is much the same: we see power block set against power block, nation against nation, party against party, opinions against other opinions, and individuals against other individuals.

We often read of attacks, of aeroplanes hijacked, banks robbed and bombs thrown in places where many innocent and unarmed people will be killed. Disorder springs up everywhere, the revolution is proclaimed as the only remedy for the ills of society, and young people are brought up to believe in violence.

In the midst of all this anarchical, senseless confusion, renewed reconciliation among men would be the most desirable, the most necessary music. The Jubilee seeks to contribute a great deal to this dynamic idea: 'Reconcile yourselves first with God,' it says, 'renewing your hearts, putting love where there is hatred, serenity where there is anger, moderate, healthy desires where there is unbridled lust.

'Once you have renewed and changed yourselves within, look outside you with new eyes and you will find a different world.'

*   *   *

It is curious, dear Casella, how the same world with the very same things in it, with the same surroundings and the same inhabitants, may become completely different when reconciliation, love and peace, which at present are missing, are brought into it.

Let me tell you the story of a Korean general. You, as an expert in harmony, will understand it very well. He died and was judged and assigned to Paradise, but when he came up before St Peter he thought of something he would like to do. He wanted to peep into Hell for a moment, just to have an idea of it. 'Right you are,' said St Peter.

So the general peeped in at the door of Hell and saw an enormous hall. In it were a number of long tables with bowls of rice on them—well-flavoured, smelling delicious, inviting. The guests were sitting there hungrily, opposite one another, each with a bowl of rice. What was happening? The guests all had chopsticks, but these were so long that, however hard they tried, not a grain of rice could they get into their mouths. And this was their torment, this was Hell. 'I've seen it, that's quite enough for me,' said the general and went back to the gates of Heaven, where he went in.

Inside, he saw the same hall, the same tables, the same rice and the same long chopsticks. But the guests were cheerful, all of them smiling and laughing. Each one, having put the food onto his chopsticks, held it out to the mouth of his companion opposite, and so they managed to eat perfectly well. Thinking of others instead of oneself had solved the problem and transformed Hell into Heaven. This is a true fable, dear Casella. Manzoni said that instead of being happy we should think of doing good, so that everyone might be better.

LUIGI CORNARO (1467?–1566), a celebrated Venetian nobleman who lived a very long life as a result of dietary methods invented by himself, which he described in a book called *Discourse on the Sober Life* (*Discorsi della vita sobria*) (1558). His advice can still persuade old people that their life can be serene and usefully employed. Cornaro was also a well-known architect:

To Luigi Cornaro

Dear nonogenarian Venetian,

Why am I writing to you? Because you were a charming Venetian four hundred years ago. Because, through a little book, which has been widely read because of its delightful ingenousness, you encouraged the sober life. And above all because you were the model of a gentle old man.

Until the age of forty you suffered from a 'very cold, damp' stomach, from 'pain in the hip', 'twinges of gout', and a hundred other ills. One fine day you flung away all your medicines. You had discovered that 'the man who wants to eat well, should eat little' and you turned over to sobriety.

Having got your health back, you were able to dedicate yourself to study, to agriculture and hydraulics, to drainage, to artistic patronage, to architecture; always good-humoured and healthy. Your *Discourse on the Sober Life*, written between the ages of eighty and ninety, was very successful in cheering people up and persuading even us old things that life could be serene and usefully employed.

Not many reached old age in your day. Little was known about hygiene, there were no modern conveniences; some illnesses hadn't yet been overcome, as they have been by now; there was no surgery, with the powerful methods and amazing results we know today; people didn't reach an average age of seventy, as in some countries they do now.

We old people are getting more and more numerous these days. In Italy the over-sixties form nearly a fifth of the population. We're known as the 'third age'. Just counting our numbers ought to cheer us up.

Whereas? Whereas we often let ourselves become anxious. We feel we've been thrown aside like old tyres, like cyclists outdistanced by the rest of the group. If we go and live with others, when our children get married and leave home, we feel a hole in our affective life and don't know what to cling to. When infirmities and signs of physical decay increase, we look sour. Instead

189

of concentrating on all the happy things God still allows us, we give way to melancholy, like the Venetian you would never have agreed with, who said: 'We're old and that's bad!'

Things are worse if we have to go into an old people's home. It means giving up the home we've always had and with which we've identified ourselves. Plenty of people adapt themselves and are happy in homes, but some feel like fish out of water. 'There's nothing I haven't got,' one of these people said to me. 'It might be the waiting-room of Paradise, but to me it's Purgatory in advance.'

* * *

The problems of the old are more complicated today than they were in your time, dear Cornaro, and perhaps more profoundly human; but the main remedy is still the same as yours: to react against pessimism and selfishness. Say to yourself: I may still have whole decades of life left, so I'll use them to make up for lost time and help others. I want to make the life that's left me into a great flame of love for God and my neighbour.

Perhaps you're not very strong? Well, you can at least pray. As a Christian I believe in the efficacy of prayer. Cloistered monks send prayers up to God from their monasteries, and I agree with Donoso Cortes that the world needs prayer more than battles. Well, we old people, by offering God our troubles and bearing them serenely, can have a great effect on the problems of man struggling in the world.

If we still have energy and time to spare, we can do more. Why not volunteer for good works? In some parishes retired school mistresses and ex-office workers provide very valuable assistance.

In France, to avoid being cut out of life, old people have actually organized themselves. 'There are spontaneous groups of young people everywhere,' they said to themselves. 'Let's form spontaneous groups of old people!' A really important movement has grown out of this, with a bishop working for it. It promotes friendship and spirituality among its members, provides help for other old people, pulls many of them out of isolation and hopelessness and sometimes brings out unsuspected, sleeping talents in a quite explosive way.

You're not the only one, dear Cornaro, to write a book after the age of eighty. Goethe finished his *Faust* at the age of eighty-one. Titian painted his self-portrait when he was over ninety. Besides, we're old only to those who come after us; to those growing old beside us we're still young. There's a kind of sliding scale for computing the years, after all. When Gounod composed his *Faust* at forty he was asked what age Faust was supposed to be in the first act. 'The usual age of the old,' replied Gounod. 'Sixty.' Twenty years later, when he himself was sixty, he was asked the same question. 'Faust is supposed to be the usual age of the old,' he answered. 'Eighty.'

* * *

At this point I can very easily look ahead and see that this letter, which is written to you, dear Cornaro, in order that others may read it, won't interest young readers. 'It's all about old fogeys,' they'll say to themselves, feeling bored. But won't they be old themselves one day? And if there's an art and a method in growing old well, then wouldn't it be a good idea for them to learn these in good time? When I was a young student, my teacher of canon law, when he came to the duties of cardinals, metropolitans and bishops, said: 'Well, those aren't very common, so we'll skip them. If any of you happen to reach these offices you can study them for yourselves.' So when I became a bishop and a metropolitan I had to start from scratch.

Now, very few young theological students will become cardinals, but nearly all today's youngsters will reach old age, and they have a duty to learn the art of growing old as they approach it, and then to keep it in reserve. If, when he's twenty, a young man grumbles 20% of the time, at seventy he's sure to grumble 70% of the time if he doesn't correct it in time, so he'd better hurry up and sweeten his nature.

Quite apart from this, it's not a bad idea for the young to realize that their problems aren't the only ones, and that the old who live side by side with them have very delicate problems

to put up with as well. To Timothy, a young bishop, St Paul said: 'Rebuke not an elder, but entreat him as a father.'

Admittedly I've been thinking mostly of us old people this time, because we need understanding and encouragement. And this, dear Cornaro, is really what you wrote yourself. And it is similar to the advice given by the editor of a daily newspaper to his contributors. 'You should often write for the old,' he told them. 'If you happen to find someone very long lived (say a man approaching a hundred with his mind entirely lucid and his faculties and strength still fresh and in good order), then don't just ignore it: put it in, give us some good news for a change! You'll have a big audience of old people who'll be delighted and will exclaim: "Now, there's a well-informed newspaper!"'

I'll be delighted if someone says: 'There, isn't the *Messaggero di S. Antonio* well informed!'

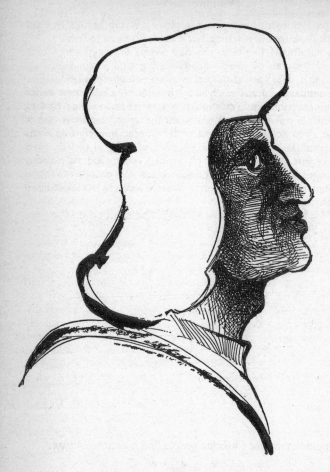

ALDUS MANUZIO, Italian printer, scholar and publisher (1450–1515).
In 1494 he set up the Aldine Press in Venice which later became famous
for the elegance of the letters he invented, known as 'italic' or 'aldine',
and for the fine editions of the classics he printed.

To Aldus Manuzio

Illustrious typographer and humanist,
I've just got back from a quick visit to the exhibition called
'Venice—City of the Book'. I was shown some very interesting
things, but I lingered with most enjoyment at the show-case of
books brought out by your famous press at the beginning of the
sixteenth century.

Once again I admired your clear slender letters, slanting
towards the right. I saw your coat of arms, with an anchor and
a dolphin and the motto *festina lente*. There were a hundred and
fifty printers and bookshops in Venice in the sixteenth century,
between the Rialto and San Marco, but yours was the best of all.
You worked for love of art and culture and died almost poor,
while colleagues of yours made fortunes; like Nicolas Jenson, of
whom Marin Sanudo wrote that 'he printed a great deal of
money'.

I didn't like seeing a book of yours side by side with a pirated
edition from the Florentine printer Giunta, who copied you
rather roughly in Lyons, damaging you by plagiarism and dishonest competition. Even when we look at four-hundred-year-old
books we can, alas, see signs of dirty tricks and the love of money.

The way old readers behaved can be seen, too. When I went
to look at the eighteenth-century books of another famous
printer, Remondini, the guide told me this man published a
translation of Lesage's novel *Gil Blas*, and it was stolen in a flash;
he also brought out the *New Flower of Virtue* and the *Christian's
Day* and the bookshops wrote to him: 'No one steals them.'
You'd think we were in the twentieth century. It's a fact that
human nature and Christian people find it hard to change.

*   *   *

Dear Manuzio, I'd love you to see a modern printing press.
Your hand-press printed three hundred sheets a day; today's
rotary presses turn out tens of thousands of newspapers in an hour.

In your day, books were so valuable that they were chained to library shelves. Few people owned them, popes excommunicated those who stole them.

Today, tons of newspapers that have been read are thrown away. In America young readers don't even deign to keep books: they buy them and as they read tear out the pages they have finished and throw them away. When they reach the end all that's left is the cover, and they throw that away too.

Then they can't be worth much, you'll say of these books. Well, some are good, some are empty, and some are very bad. In comparison with the bad ones, *Polifilo*, which you printed— the most beautiful book in the world from a typographical point of view—seems a nun's prayer-book.

As you were a humanist, you'll no doubt remember Chapter 3 of Book 8 of Plato's *Republic*. In this he lists the signs of democratic decadence: governments are supported by their people only on condition that they authorize the worst excesses; the man who obeys the law is called a fool; fathers are afraid to correct their children; children outrage their parents ('to be free', Plato observes ironically); the master is afraid of his pupil and the pupil despises his master; the young behave as if they were old and the old tell funny stories to imitate the young; women dress to look like men, and so on. Well, you know the chapter.

In some of our books today what Plato considered shameful and treated ironically is treated seriously, sometimes actually used in a religious context.

Are youngsters impatient to develop their sexuality? Chastity is repressive, it's said; it favours capitalism and medievalism, it's out of date and we must have a sexual revolution. Is a new life beginning in sad circumstances in a woman's body? These clever churchmen make a distinction between human life and humanized life. Human life which is not yet humanized can be interrupted without scruple, they say.

Do children disobey? Well, parents no longer give orders or bother their little darlings. Do schoolchildren no longer learn their lessons? A quite simple answer: get rid of lessons. The school of life is quite enough without the mediation of teachers, because it isn't by learning subjects that children are educated, but by discussing social problems.

Are students fed up with marks and classifications? Away with classifications. They're discriminatory, unworthy of an egalitarian society. Does a student wish to study medicine? No-one's going to stop him if he's signed on—exams or no exams, study or no study—for six years at university.

I'll say no more about other amazing declarations that would make the hair of a humanist like you stand on end. I'd also like you to see something of newspapers and magazines, all things that in your day existed only in a very rudimentary sort of way. In the Campiello San Giacometo there was, and in fact there still is, a statue known as the Rialto Dwarf, on which were hung bits of paper, blown about and containing jokes and small news items, which people went to read, full of curiosity. It was a miniature newspaper with mini-readers.

I wish you could see the queues around newspaper kiosks today. If you were to read some of the illustrated weeklies, which are sometimes full of indecent matters, and could make a practice of reading the daily papers, you'd see that we've gone a long way from the days of the Rialto Dwarf! No longer are they small, occasional sheets: news pours out in a flood over people every day, without any delay.

The Republic of Venice boasted that within three months it could get to know what was happening throughout the Mediterranean. Today we see the astronauts at the very moment in which they land on the moon, from only a yard's distance.

News, unfortunately, almost overwhelms us, so frequent is it, and so abundant. It leaves us no time to reflect, and we are so bewildered that gradually we aren't surprised by anything, and aren't even able to enjoy what's beautiful.

We must also take account of the pressures upon us. I'll try and give you an idea of them. In America there are university chairs of 'publicity'; they teach people to take account of the psychology of consumers, working directly on the nervous system of the individual and on his inferiority complex, till he is brought to the following dilemma: either I buy such-and-such a product, or I'm condemned to hopeless misery.

In a magazine advertisement, for instance, we are shown an attractive girl, Rachel. She is pretty, but, at parties, nobody asks her to dance. Why? She finds out for herself when she overhears a conversation. 'Rachel really ought to ask a dentist about her breath!' The dentist is consulted at once. 'This isn't a problem,' he tells her. 'All you need do is use such-and-such toothpaste.' Rachel uses it, and here she is again, happy, courted and admired. This is typical of the consumer society. I mentioned commercial advertising, but I might also have mentioned other cases involving politics and the trade unions, in which ideological propaganda and secret persuaders are at work.

* * *

So, dear Manuzio, today we look less at the printers and more at those responsible for the newspapers. If only they had your professional delicacy! The passion for news oughtn't to make them forget that they have a duty of charity and justice towards private people, who are generally defenceless in the face of the press and of society. We can't react to a newspaper that attacks us like the statesman Thiers, who said: 'Let them write! I'm an old umbrella on which insults have been pouring for forty years. A drop more or less is all the same to me.'

In Venice you had censorship, which controlled your books. Today there's virtually none. If only there was a little self-censorship! Admittedly a great deal also depends on the readers. If they showed they had more serious tastes, self-censorship would function at once and even the newspapers would become more serious. It's well known that a people gets the newspapers it deserves and desires.

Will this happen? Let's hope so.

But for the present, if you were here, your heart would be torn to see the great mountain of bad publications and the small pile of good ones. It's a problem that Catholics—if they really are Catholics—should make real efforts to solve.

The Germans have a saying: 'The cow's thin. Do you expect it to give plenty of milk? Then give it more hay!'

ST BONAVENTURE (1221–74) known as 'the Seraphic Doctor', General of the Franciscan Order, bishop and cardinal, a speaker much listened to at the Council at Lyons, and a prolific writer on theology and mysticism. His thought was centred on the figure of Christ the Saviour, and culminated in his doctrine on the 'Journey of the Mind to God'.

Mark Twain, when he was editor of a newspaper, didn't confine himself to writing and getting people to write, but put out propaganda through every possible means. One day a picture of a donkey at the bottom of a well appeared on the first page. The caption said: 'I wonder why this poor donkey is dead at the bottom of a well?' A few days later the picture reappeared and the caption said: 'The poor donkey is dead because he did not call for help.'

Dear Manuzio! I am that donkey. And I'm calling for help in getting a better press.

To St Bonaventure

Learned Saint,

The Franciscans are preparing a great celebration for the seven hundredth anniversary of your death (1274 to 1974).

What aspects of your personality will they stress?

You were first a student, then a teacher at the University of Paris; you were head of the Franciscan Order, bishop and cardinal, an influential speaker at the ecumenical council of Lyons, and a writer of theological and mystical works that achieved great fame in the centuries after your death.

What will the friars emphasize about you? I don't know. If it was up to me, I'd choose the *Life of St Francis* from among all your books, and make it known to a large audience. It is a masterpiece, in literary terms as well as others. Your mind was deeply involved as you wrote it, in a style that is at the same time elevated and picturesquely fanciful. While you were writing it your friend St Thomas enjoyed its fine qualities and said: 'Let's have a saint writing about another saint.' I like to think he was foreseeing the great spiritual fruit it would bear.

I bet, though, neither you nor he would have foreseen the interpretation made by a university student who was talking to me the other day. 'We, today's young people,' he said, 'are with Saint Francis.' 'That's good,' I said. 'Yes,' he went on, 'just as St Francis stood up to his father and flung his clothes in his face, so we fling all it's given us, or rather all it's imposed on us, in the face of this filthy consumer society of ours!'

When you were studying in Paris as a plain layman, there were ten thousand university students there. They argued noisily, were riotous, and often challenged authority. But in a different way.

The style and problems of our young challengers today are different. Let me tell you something about them.

* * *

'All authority is repression'

Even in your day, the young wanted to bring in innovations and so get away from the past. But today they—or many of them, at least—want a complete break with the past. They reject society as a whole, the family, marriage, school, morals and religion.

'You want to throw everything out,' I said to the young man I've just mentioned. 'But what comes later? What are you going to put in place of the institutions you've knocked down?'

'That's a bourgeois question,' he replied.

That's the trouble. Our young people protest, but they don't suggest.

You may say: 'Maybe these are poor, disinherited youngsters, and that's why they hate the bourgeoisie.' Oh no, they're the children of the bourgeoisie themselves, they very often have everything. They have plenty to live on, but no ideals to live by.

'But there must be some excuses to explain this situation?' you'll say. Certainly there are, I'll try and put down some of them.

Today, higher education and the universities have been flung open to all. Hundreds of thousands of young people receive higher education in Italy every year. But they don't find what they ought to find there and besides, there's no relation between the possibility of studying at an advanced level and the possibility of getting the right job.

Young people with degrees or diplomas can't find adequate jobs and the number of unemployed intellectuals is going to increase enormously during the next few years. Society didn't foresee this trouble, which is a very serious one, and young people take it out on society.

That's not all. There's a terrible moral and religious void in this same society. Today, everyone seems to be after material advancement: everyone wants to earn, to invest, to surround himself with further comforts, to do well. Few think of doing good.

God, who should take over our lives, has become a distant star, to be looked at only at particular times. People think they're religious because they go to church, thinking that once they're outside the church they can lead a life just like that of so many other people, filled with all kinds of dirty tricks—large or small—with injustices, with sins against charity; in other words a life that's totally inconsistent.

The young, who want consistency, won't stand for it. They find inconsistencies, real or apparent, in the Church itself, and so they reject her as well. And as they've got to believe in something, they support appalling fashionable ideologies and the wayward cult of sex which, under the name of 'sexual or erotic liberation', is an upside-down sort of religion as well.

And that's not all. There's the cult of freedom. But it's not the classic freedom to do what you must without being bothered or to be able to choose between one thing and another. No, it's absolute independence. 'I'm the only one to decide what's good and what's bad. I want to realize myself without depending on any law from outside. Anyone who stands up to my wishes attacks my personality. All authority is repression. Every structure's a prison, everyone in authority's a cop'

You, wisest and gentlest of saints, taught for many years, and teaching seemed to you a service to truth, to the students and to their families. If you were to return today! The very fact that you were a teacher would mean that you were regarded as a 'mandarin' or a 'snob', trying to force his own culture on the students in order to chain them to the 'system'.

You'd hear talk of 'de-schooling'. 'If there have to be schools,' you'd be told, 'then the students oughtn't to learn particular subjects, but should become used to discussing present-day political problems.' You'd have to accept the 'social role' of the school, and have to deal not just with the students and their parents but with the political parties and the trade unions. The time for preparing lessons would partly be gobbled up by long meetings and discussions.

This isn't entirely bad—not at all. Dialogue with the young is quite right and proper, and it's only fair that the various social components should be involved in the school. The school should be alive, and should avoid the dreary, exaggerated emphasis it once laid on the learning of facts and abstractions. It's only the excesses of the present trends that spoil things.

Are these youngsters pitiless towards their teachers, then? I would say yes. But they are equally pitiful towards the poor, the outcast, and the excluded, and that's good. They say they are against all social divisions, all discrimination of class and race. This is fine and generous. In this field, alas, they are also faced with grave injustices, against which they rebel.

They hear of nations that call themselves Christian and still allow torture in order to strike at ideas. They see workers' families forced to live on very little while a few get amazingly rich, no one knows how.

In a single evening a singer can earn a fortune and by selling records of her songs can become a millionaire. They read of aid to the Third World, and realize it's only a trifle. A great deal more is spent on armaments, while the Third World continues to suffer and to die.

There really is a good deal to be indignant about. But this righteous contempt of the young is deliberately worked up by painting our own societies with even darker and more sinister colours than need be, and keeping quiet about the monstrous iniquities of other societies, which are shown, instead, as models, even as earthly paradises.

* * *

But I don't want to make things look too dark myself. Not all our young people are like that. Many of them are hardworking, respectful, and preparing themselves seriously for life. Unfortunately, while the others talk and write, they are silent. Those who protest often expect a great deal from adult protesters, and are disappointed when they are given vague replies and told that such-and-such a thing is being 'looked into'.

We must make concrete suggestions to them. *Freedom?* But, without God, what freedom? Progress and knowledge tell us more and more *how* this world is made. Only Christ's doctrine tells us *why* we are in it.

A model? Christ is the right choice, for ever, for everyone. He went along a particular road and said 'Follow me'. The road was a bit narrow, but it was the way of loyalty and love for all, on which the poor and unimportant were privileged; a way that led to the 'Father's glory'. On the cross, he offered himself to the Father; in raising him from the dead the Father declared that he had accepted the offer, and glorified his humanity and that of all who are his, joyfully proclaiming that the whole world would one day be transformed into 'a new heaven and a new earth'.

A world to be improved? The struggle for justice and for the removal of the causes of evil? Certainly, but let each man begin by improving himself. And let's be careful not to fall into naive notions of Utopia. Any system will always have its imperfections. Let's not judge others, and give them no right of appeal. Let's not divide them radically into the good all on one side, the bad on the other; loyalty here, tyranny there; this is progressive, that's conservative. Life is always much more complex. The good lack certain qualities, the bad have some virtues.

A faithless Church? That's what the Fathers called it. But they

205

were more precise: they called it the *holy* faithless Church. As it's made up of sinners, it follows that the Church itself is sinful, but it still gives useful help and provides examples of sanctity to all who trust her. We must see, too, whether all that she's accused of is true. The Church these writers (perhaps in good faith) have in mind is unlike the real Church, unlike the way it really is outside their minds.

*   *   *

Gentle St Bonaventure, the contemporaries who were lucky enough to hear you were delighted with what you said. 'He spoke with an angel's tongue,' they said. I wish you could speak like an angel today: particularly to parents, educators, politicians, all those responsible for the young. And I'd like you to say: 'Don't be afraid of any effort, any just reform, any expense, any dialogue, so long as it helps these youngsters. It's for their good, but for yours as well. Anyone who's afraid of effort and expense today may pay dearly for it tomorrow.'

Tolstoy could have emphasized these final words with a parable.

In the little principality of Monaco the judges years ago condemned a villain to the guillotine, but then realized they had neither the guillotine nor the hangman they needed. Monaco was such a small principality! They asked for both from their neighbour France, but when they heard what it would cost to rent them they were alarmed. 'Too expensive,' they cried. They asked the King of Sardinia for a similar loan, but once again it was too expensive.

So they left the villain in prison. But the warder, the cook, and the prisoner's food all added up. 'Let's open the prison and let him get on with it!' the judges decided.

When he saw the door was open, the prisoner went out for a walk along the shore. But at midday he went along to the prince's kitchen to claim his meal. This went on and on—for two days, three days, four . . . It threatened to become expensive for the principality again, and so it was decided to speak to the man. 'Don't you realize you're to go?' they said. 'All right, I'll go,' said the man, 'but you've got to pay me.' And they·had to pay up. So, because it was all 'too expensive' and they kept putting things off, a brigand was once again loose in the world, to go about committing further crimes.

Let's never say 'it's too expensive', unless we want the brigand of savage, revolutionary opposition to wander about the world. Let's not put off solving problems, let's not put off spending, or getting involved in dialogue. Let's talk to these youngsters and try to help them with new methods suited to the times, but with the same deep love that you had, dear saint, when you helped them in your own day.

CHRISTOPHER MARLOWE, English dramatist and poet (1564–93), who ranks second only to Shakespeare for dramatic power and development of blank verse. His best-known works are *Tamburlaine the Great*, *Edward II*, *The Jew of Malta* and *Doctor Faustus*, which tells the story of the Wittenberg doctor who sells his soul to the devil.

To Christopher Marlowe

Illustrious poet,

I came across you for the first time when I was reading the poet Carducci.

Carducci writes that he was travelling in a carriage along the Chiarone, a small river in the Maremma in Tuscany: the 'lean' horses run on, the darkness increases, a light rain falls and the poet is reading your book. He must have had some disturbing visions from it because he writes:

> 'From the cruel, ferocious verse,
> like the dream of a man
> with much beer weighing upon him
> ... comes a bitter vapour
> of awesome sadness'

Then suddenly he can't bear it any longer and flings your book away.

'Away with you, Marlowe, into the water!'

I was then a boy. Of course I wondered: 'What can be so awesome and fierce in that book? I can't go and fish it up out of the Chiarone, but maybe I can find it in the library.'

I found it: *The Tragedy of Dr Faustus*.

And it really is tragic and dark. In the first pages I found the terms of the contract between Faust and the devil:

'First that Faustus may be a spirit in form and substance. Secondly, that Mephistopheles shall be his servant and at his command. Thirdly, that Mephistopheles shall do for him, and bring him whatsoever he wishes. Fourthly, that he shall be in his chamber or house invisible. Lastly, that he shall appear to the said John Faustus at all times in whatever form or shape he please. I, John Faustus, of Wertenberg, doctor, by these presents, do give both body and soul to Lucifer Prince of the East, and his minister Mephistopheles; and furthermore grant unto them, that, twenty-four years being expired, the articles above written inviolate, full power to fetch or carry the said John Faustus,

body and soul, flesh, blood, or goods, into their habitation wheresoever.

By me, John Faustus.'

When I came to the end of the play I said to myself: 'Marlowe was wonderful as a poet of the horrible, but isn't the devil stupid and isn't the doctor mad to make a contract like that?'

Today I can answer: 'Yes, the devil was stupid, the doctor was mad, and it's lucky the contract never existed!' But others interrupt me at this point and say: 'The lucky thing is that the devil doesn't exist!'

I don't suppose this modern denial of the devil is of much interest to you, Marlowe. You were inclined to deny his existence yourself, if I've understood you rightly, four hundred and fifty years ago. And I'm very sorry about it.

With Charles Baudelaire, who like you was a poet and like you anything but a pious fellow, I think 'the devil's most successful trick is to make men believe he does not exist'. The devil is one of the main characters of history, yet he tries to pass largely unknown through the world and to make men deny his existence, so that they will carry on his own revolt against God; and in this he has been, to some extent, successful.

This was proved a few months ago, when the Pope spoke sternly about the devil, saying he existed not merely as impersonal evil but as a real person—invisible, admittedly, but active and busy in his task of damaging mankind.

What an outcry followed! People in high positions in newspapers and reviews suddenly turned into theologians and made condescending statements, saying that what the Pope had said couldn't be taken seriously, that it was reviving medieval myths and damaging 'progressive' theology, which today confined the devil to the tiny corner in which he had a 'cultural' place.

A book actually appeared called *The Pope and the Devil*. You, Marlowe, would have called him a *malignantis naturae*; but in that book he was really just an excuse. Pope Paul's service to the Church and to the world is its real subject, treated with an apparently sober list of facts and objective research. Beneath this is a sometimes total incapacity to understand Church matters, a sometimes amateurish naivety, and a sometimes unpleasant amount of bias.

More positive was the reaction of some 'broadminded' theologians. When they were questioned, they clenched their teeth and said a Catholic could hardly deny the devil's existence with any decency, since he was spoken of so openly in the Bible.

*   *   *

This is the point: the Bible and its proper reading. There's a surprising thing about it: while the ancient religions of the East had a highly developed and picturesque demonology, the Old Testament gives the devil very short shrift. Perhaps the writers of the Bible were afraid of damaging monotheisim, of harming official Jewish culture, or of falsifying the problem of evil.

He turns up more often in the New Testament. Devils are called demons, spirits, evil spirits, impure spirits, the evil one, the tempter. These spirits—according to the Gospel—try to oppose the coming of the Kingdom, and tempt man as they tempted Jesus in the desert.

St John sees the passion of Jesus as a fight against the devil. In the Acts it is said that the Apostles' preaching will be the continuation of the struggle between the Kingdom of God and the kingdom of the devil.

Several times both Jesus and his listeners blame the devil for illnesses: blindness, dumbness, deafness, convulsions, mental handicaps. Jesus cures these illnesses, but never through magic formulas or exorcism. He simply gives an order or makes a simple gesture.

Paul often speaks of the power of the devil and of temptation, which he says is frequent, varied and harmful. The devil will turn himself into an angel of light the better to deceive Christians. Paul himself is slapped by an 'angel of Satan' in attacks that are no more exactly described. But he isn't frightened: the powers of darkness cannot separate him from the love of Christ. Jesus—he says—has freed us from the power of the devil and it is the Christians whom the angels will judge, in the end.

More highly-coloured is the book of the Apocalypse. To be quite honest, its demonology isn't easy to interpret. It is set against the fight between angels and devils, and the victory of the angels. The early centuries of Christianity were influenced by the Apocalypse and their demonology often contained the idea of cunning. God hid his divinity under the human nature of Christ, and the devil flung himself incautiously upon him. Hooked like a stupid fish, says St Gregory, the Pope. Caught like a greedy mouse in the trap of the cross, says St Augustine. St Cyril of Jerusalem speaks of poison, which the devil swallows; it then makes him spit out the souls he's kept imprisoned.

This idea of the devil as a trickster tricked was later abandoned by theologians but taken up by artists. You didn't like it, Marlowe, and made poor Faust end up in Mephistopheles's claws for ever; but Dante liked it and so did Goethe.

In Dante we have Buonconte di Montefeltro, excommunicated and quite certainly a victim of the devil, who is expecting to seize him. But before dying Buonconte thinks of calling on the Madonna. The angel of God then has the right to snatch up his soul and the devil, tricked and disappointed, can only scream angrily up to him: 'Oh, you from heaven, why take him from me?'

In Goethe, poor Mephistopheles, after working for many years to satisfy Faust's desires in youth and age, is tricked nonetheless. At the last minute whole choirs of angels come down from heaven to fight off the forces of the devil and save Faust.

'The soul I was promised . . .
was stolen through a trick!'

Mephistopheles shouts contemptuously.

But whatever Mephistopheles may say, God doesn't trick anyone. It's the devil and his followers who are tricksters.

This is the dominant theme of the demonology of the Fathers who fled to the desert in the early centuries of the Church. They don't consider the desert as a shelter from the corruption of the world and a place where God speaks in solitude and in a special way to the heart of man. Not at all: it's a battlefield where men go alone to stand up to the devil and beat him, as Jesus did. According to the Fathers, devils considered the desert their own dominion. 'Get out of our house!' they shouted at St Anthony, and put a thousand pitfalls in his way to stop him passing and disturbing their last refuge by filling it with monks.

The nasty jokes they played are famous and were a daily occurrence in the lives of all the hermits. Pious pilgrims who went to visit the Fathers of the Desert heard them with amazement. St Pacomius knelt down to pray and the devil dug a hole under him; he was working and the devil suddenly appeared before him in the form of a cock, who crowed under his nose; he was praying and a wolf or a vixen jumped on him, snarling. St Macarius, travelling to a temple of some idol, poked sticks into the sand along the road in order to find his way back; while he was asleep the devil pulled all the sticks up and Macarius found them in a bundle under his head, like a pillow.

Spiteful, provoking, envious tempters, these devils were. But if a monk watched and prayed he could gain complete victory over them. These aren't true stories, of course, so much as books intended to teach or point moral lessons. Yet they were read and believed as history, making a deep impression upon simple believers and giving rise to other books and other beliefs.

In the Middle Ages it was still thought that the devil came especially to torment the holiest people, in guises that were sometimes frightening and sometimes disturbing. If a poor nun longed for a basket of salad, Satan was lurking in the basket. If a monk enjoyed having a bird to sing in his lonely cell, then Satan was in its song. Satan can be found lurking even in the illuminated miniatures in prayer books, in pictures painted above altars, or in the very rope that went round the monk's waist, over his habit.

Worse still was Satan who, as an incubus, raped virgins and put accursed children into their wombs. Medieval religion, alas, very often lapsed into superstition in such matters. Robert, Duke of Normandy, was nicknamed the Devil, since he was thought to have been fathered by the devil.

In spite of the Church's efforts, magic was often linked and allied with demonology. Sorceresses and witches and poisoners were believed in right up to the sixteenth and seventeenth centuries. It was thought that these women could use the powers of hell against enemies, and that they flew off at night to take part in the sabbaths of Satan.

How can all this be explained? Not merely by calling it wickedness, for often it was believed through ignorance and good faith. Let us say, then, that it was for the following reasons: the ingenuousness of writers, who accepted facts without checking them as they should have done; the easy credulity of people who rashly mixed the word of God with superstitious manifestations; and psychological and pathological happenings, which were seen with a superficially religious eye instead of a scientific one.

Rejecting these exaggerations and errors does not mean rejecting everything, however.

The fact that the devil exists, as a pure invisible spirit, can be no more of a problem than the existence of God and the angels. To admit his power over human beings cannot make us afraid, if we believe in the victory won by Christ. On the cross Christ seemed defeated. Whereas he was the victor and this was seen in the Resurrection.

We find ourselves in the same situation: subjected to so many temptations, tests and sufferings that we seem defeated: but with the grace of Our Lord we shall be victors!

St Luke wrote the Third Gospel and the Acts of the
Apostles. He lived in the first century AD and was a
physician and a close friend of St Paul, with whom
he collaborated and whose third missionary journey
he shared. Although he did not see the life of Christ
with his own eyes, his contribution to the New
Testament is unique, particularly in what he wrote
about the childhood of Christ.

To St Luke the Evangelist

Dear St Luke,

I've always liked you! You were all gentleness, a man who sought reconciliation.

In your Gospel you emphasized Christ's infinite goodness, and the fact that sinners were especially loved by God, that Jesus almost ostentatiously involved himself with those who enjoyed no consideration in this world.

Only you gave an account of the birth and infancy of Christ, which we hear read with renewed emotion every Christmas. A short phrase of yours strikes me in particular: 'Wrapped in swaddling clothes and laid in a manger.' This has given rise to all the cribs in the world and to thousands of wonderful paintings. I'll add a verse from the Breviary to it:

> He accepted to lie in the hay,
> he had no fear of the manger.
> He who feeds the least of the birds,
> was nourished with a little milk.

Having done this, I say to myself: 'Christ took the humblest position. What position do we take?'

Let me tell you the answers I've found to this question. Before God, our position is that of Abraham: 'Behold now, I have taken upon me to speak unto the Lord, which am but dust and ashes.' Or else that of the publican who, on the threshold of the Temple, far from the altar, dared not raise his eyes to heaven when he thought of the sins he had committed.

Before an infinite and omnipotent God we must accept that we are very small, and repress in ourselves any tendency that is contrary to proper submissiveness. God, as it happens, wishes to be imitated by us in some things, while in others he wants to be unique and inimitable. He says: 'Learn from me for I am meek and humble', 'Be merciful as your heavenly father is merciful'. But he also says: 'Honour and glory are to God alone' and 'Only God is the absolute and independent.'

We try to overturn this position. We wish to have autonomy, independence and honours for ourselves; we don't wish to be the least bit dependent, mild and patient. If need be, we back ourselves up with the 'new philosophies' (which will soon be old philosophies) and with Culture with a capital C. Progress has gone to our heads: we are highly conscious of having been to the moon, of having set up a consumer civilization with every possible comfort.

But just as we were forgetting Him from whom comes every gift of mind and energy, the Middle Eastern sheiks reminded us harshly and abruptly. 'Look, you rich consumer countries, the party's over,' they said. 'There's now only enough oil for another thirty years. Anyone who wants it must pay a high price. You must reorganize yourselves entirely, and look for other sources of energy.'

This reminder, and the hard times ahead, may be good for us. On the one hand they stimulate us to new research and to finding new ways to progress; on the other, they remind us of the limits of all that is earthly and of our duty to place our highest hopes only in God.

I have heard a 'Christian critic' say: 'We've had enough of *petit bourgeois* religion, which talks of paradise and saving individual souls. All that stinks of capitalist individualism and takes the attention of the poor away from the great social problems. Anyone who preaches the Gospel must speak of whole peoples, of the masses, of the salvation of all. Christ came to free the people from their exile in capitalist civilization, and to lead them into the promised land of the new society that is about to be born.'

The only thing that's true in that is the idea that the Christian should occupy himself with important social problems, and do something effective about them. The more we long for heaven, the more we should help to establish justice on earth. As for the rest, civilization, whether capitalist or socialist, is only temporary for each one of us; we live in it only on our way through this world.

Our true country is Paradise. Led by Christ, we are all going there, together, yet each of us with his individual destiny.

Anyone who doesn't believe in it is unfortunate: he is 'without hope', as St Paul would say, and hasn't yet found the deepest meaning of his existence. Towards our neighbour, we are in three positions, depending on whether we are dealing with our superiors, our equals, or our inferiors.

But can we speak of superiors nowadays? Can we still say: children should love, respect and obey their parents, pupils their teachers, citizens the authorities?

In the seventeenth century, here in Venice, the famous Carnival took place. People seemed to go mad during those days, did whatever they wanted, and—hidden behind masks— gave vent to their feelings against laws and customs, almost as if they were getting their own back for the months spent being obedient and well behaved. I have a feeling that something similar is happening today.

I'm not so much afraid when I hear that there are attacks, robberies, kidnappings and murders all over the world. These have always existed. More frightening is the new way in which many people now look at them. The law, and standards of behaviour, are considered things to joke about, or else they are considered repressive, alienating. People love hearing anything bad about the law. The only thing prohibited today—it is said— is prohibition, and anyone who tries to forbid anything looks as if he belongs to the old, out-dated 'oppressive society'. Some magistrates, when they pass sentence, give the impression that they are quite arbitrarily opening a gap in the hedge of the law, and the forces whose task it is to make public order respected are often mocked.

Even in clerical circles, ecclesiastical laws are thrown out one after another in a surprisingly lighthearted way. Inquiries— more or less scientific—are held which all seem to conclude with something like this: 'Dear people, you are unhappy with the present situation; if you want to be happy, change everything and overthrow the present structures.'

Psychology, a science that explains all human behaviour, is also brought in. And what happens? Adulterers, sadists and homosexuals are nearly always forgiven by psychologists. The fault lies with their parents, who didn't love their little darlings as they should. A whole literature has appeared that has 'Take it out on the father!' for its theme; making the father responsible for pretty well everything. Another, propagating complete freedom from every law, demands unlimited contraception, abortion on demand, divorce at will, premarital relations, homosexuality and the use of drugs.

It is a tidal wave, a kind of cyclone that is advancing, dear St Luke; and in the face of it what is a poor bishop to do? He may concede that the law has often been too absolute in the past, that it was made into a kind of altar upon which the individual was too often sacrificed. He may see that sometimes it is the parents themselves who have removed all restraints from their children ('I don't want my child to undergo the sort of strictness I had to suffer'). He can admit that the same parents have sometimes forgotten the warning: 'Fathers, provoke not your children to anger, lest they be discouraged' (Col. 3, 21). He knows perfectly well that the exercise of all authority is a service and must be carried out like a service. He remembers the words of St Peter: 'As free, and not using your liberty for a cloak of maliciousness, but as the servants of God.' These words make no mention of what is called power, and claim an authority that promotes freedom; they don't ask for a servile obedience, but for one that is adult, active and responsible.

And after that? After that, a bishop must trust in God, firmly remembering the divine words: 'He who fears God honours the father . . . My son, with your words and deeds honour your father.' 'Children, obey your parents in all things: for this is well pleasing to the Lord' (Col. 3, 20). 'Let every soul be subject unto the higher powers. For there is no power but of God: the powers that be are ordained of God. Whosoever therefore resisteth the power, resisteth the ordinance of God.' (Rom. 13, 1–2). 'I exhort therefore that, first of all, supplications, prayers, intercessions, and giving of thanks, be made for all men; For kings, and for all that are in authority.' (1 Tim. 2, 1–2); 'Obey them that have the rule over you, and submit yourselves: for they watch for your souls, as they that must give account, that

they may do it with joy, and not with grief' (Heb. 13, 17).

*　　*　　*

Then there are our equals. In relation to them our duty is: to be simple, to avoid eccentricity and the exaggerated wish to be noticed. Sometimes our tendency is not to do what others do, but to do what others don't; to contradict whatever they say; to despise what they admire; to admire what they despise.

Some people try to stand out for the elegance, luxury, bright colours and richness of their clothes, others for their original, peculiar way of speaking. A ring on one's finger, a curl peeping out from under a brim, a feather on a mountaineer's hat, make some people incredibly pleased with themselves. These things aren't serious in themselves, of course, but they are often small ways of making ourselves noticed, of surprising other people and of masking our own mediocrity.

The plain, simple man, on the other hand, doesn't try to seem richer or more cultivated, more pious or noble or powerful than he is. Being what we should be, seeming what we are, dressing suitably for our condition, not making ourselves deliberately noticed, not putting anyone down, these are your suggestions, dear St Luke. Jesus approved of them and recommended them before you did; and then you preserved them: 'Go and sit down in the lowest room'; 'Woe unto you, Pharisees! for ye love the uppermost seats in the synagogues, and greetings in the markets.'

*　　*　　*

Finally there are our inferiors, or rather those who are more unfortunate that ourselves, because they are ill or poor or in trouble or sinners. Towards them we have the duty of positive Christian love, which must be given to everyone, and to the group or class they belong to as well.

Today I see two mistaken attitudes over this. Some people say: 'I love and help the individual who is poor and that's all; I'm not interested in "the poor" as a class'. Others say: 'I'll fight only for the entire class of poor people, for all outcasts, for the

Third World. Caring for individual cases with small acts of charity won't do, in fact it holds back the definitive revolution.'

To the first I reply: we must love positively all the poor who, united and organized together, are struggling to improve their situation. We must do as Christ did; he loved everyone, but gave the poor a special privilege, an intenser love.

To the second kind I say: it is a good thing to have chosen the cause of the poor, the outcast, the Third World. Be careful, though, that you don't make the distant, organized poor an excuse for neglecting the poor who are near you. Your mother is poor and near you: why do you disobey her and upset her? Your teacher is another of the poor who is close to you: why are you so disrespectful and pitiless towards him? And why did you hit your schoolfellow violently, to stop him coming into class with you, because his political ideas were the opposite of yours? You support the great cause of peace. Fine, but be careful that you're not doing what was done in the words of the prophet Jeremiah: 'saying, peace, peace; when there is no peace.' Peace, in fact, is expensive: it is made not with words, but with loving sacrifices and renunciations from everyone. It isn't possible to find it through human effort alone: we need the intervention of God.

It is the Christmas greeting of the angels, one of the most beautiful things, dear St Luke, that you ever set down: '. . . and on earth peace, goodwill toward men.'

MARCUS FABIUS QUINTILIAN, Roman writer of Spanish origin (c. AD 35–96) who lived in Rome under the Emperors Vespasian and Domitian. He was a lawyer, an enthusiastic educator, and he ran a prestigious school of oratory in Rome; he was also the first orator paid by the state. His main work is the *Institutio oratoria*, a valuable work on the education of boys.

To Quintilian

Illustrious Quintilian,

You were a great lawyer, an eloquent speaker, and, above all, a great and enthusiastic educator of the young.

Pliny the Younger was one of your pupils. The Emperor Domitian entrusted you with the education of his nephews, the sons of his sister, Flavia Domitilla.

The first of the twelve books of your main work, the *Institutio*, was an authoritative work from the Middle Ages until a few years ago.

I discovered it only recently, and re-read some of your maxims.

1) Let the master not expect from a child what only the adolescent can give, nor from an adolescent what is expected of an adult. When he has done well, say: 'Why, you're already someone!' And add: 'The best of you is still to come.' Thus you will encourage him, stimulate him, and open up a hopeful future to him.

2) It is not a good idea to have a single master teaching a single pupil. If he does not compare himself with others, the pupil is in danger of becoming conceited; and, set before a single pupil, the master does not give the best of himself. If there are several in the class, there is emulation and competition, and this often stimulates boys to study, more than the masters' exhortations or the parents' entreaties.

3) A spirit of criticism does not suit the young, and should not be made more important than imagination and creativity.

4) The master should not be too severe in correcting his pupils.

If he is, the timid are discouraged, fear everything and attempt nothing; the livelier pupils become angry and put up tacit resistance. Be fatherly; have no vices and do not tolerate them. Be austere but not rigid; kindly but not without energy; do not make yourself hated for your strictness or despised for your lack of energy; speak often of what is good and honest. . .

*　　*　　*

To look through these maxims again made me feel both touched and sad, so distant are they from the maxims which I read in certain modern treatises on education—works I see approved of, more or less everywhere.

1) Suppose I told you, illustrious Quintilian, that there are teachers who even in the primary schools keep talking about, and endlessly returning to, Vietnam, Chile, the Palestinians? What matters, they say, is not for the children to be given information gathered by others in the past, but for them to learn to argue about the great problems of the present.

2) Emulation, competition? These are forbidden words today. They encourage individualism, the class spirit, the meritocracy, capitalism. Marks should go not to the individual but to the group.

3) As for a spirit of criticism, it is one of the things most eagerly cultivated. Society is shown to the children in its worst aspects, sometimes very exaggeratedly, and then they are told: 'This is your target, children! Fire away!' You were afraid of tacit resistance, Quintilian. Today we have active resistance in the schools and it is anything but silent!

4) A *fatherly* master? Not on your life! Today 'paternalism' is hunted down, swept out of every corner, feared; it is synonymous with oppression, repression, authoritarianism. Today the fashionable words are: group work, school without subjects, social and democratic training enriched by meetings and demonstrations. If you came back to teach after nineteen centuries, dear Quintilian, you'd certainly have to be brought up to date!

Not that all this is bad. The four points and their slogans that

I have contrasted with your four contain the solutions of the extremists. There are intermediate positions, though, which even you, perhaps, would not dislike and with which your maxims might, with a little adaptation, go very well.

*　　*　　*

Group work, for instance, which you didn't know, is good. In the group, if it works well, there is not just the sum total of three, four or five brains, but a new stimulus which works on the intelligence of each one. I try to understand what the next in the group has already understood: his lamp lights another one in me, and this, in its turn, helps him, or a third, or a fourth.

In another way group work stimulates me to be active instead of merely receptive, to be myself in what I learn, to show my thought to others and to show it in an original way.

Not only that: there's also an exchange of experiences, which enriches others and me; friendship is strengthened in this exchange, and so is courteous attention to others.

But this doesn't exclude the master's teaching: in fact, it presupposes it. Dependence is natural to the mind, which doesn't create the truth, but must merely bow down before it, wherever it comes from. If we don't profit from the teaching of others, we waste a lot of time looking for truths that have already been discovered. It isn't always possible to make original discoveries; often it is enough to be critically certain of discoveries that have already been made. Finally, docility is a useful quality.

A university teacher realized this when the maid asked him if she could take a burning coal from the stove to use in the flat-iron. 'Go ahead,' he said, 'but where are you going to carry the coal?' 'Here,' said the maid, showing him the palm of her hand. She put a layer of cold ashes on it, placed the hot coal on top of them and went off, thanking him. 'Well,' said the professor, 'with all my knowledge, I didn't know that!'

Nor must it be thought that when we listen to a teacher we remain purely passive or receptive. Youngsters who are real scholars aren't saucepans ready to receive the soup the master pours into them, stirring vigorously with his wooden spoon. Dante, Leonardo and Galileo didn't just sit dumbly below their master's desk. St Thomas showed he wanted pupils to be very much on their toes when he said: 'The master should confine himself to "moving", to stimulating his pupil, and only if he responds to this stimulus—either during or after the master's explanation—does he arrive at real learning.'

On the other hand: is it better to be the receiver of great ideas or the originator of mediocre ones? Pascal used to say: He who has climbed on to another's shoulders will see further than the other, even if he is smaller than he is.

* * *

Giving attention to the weakest in the school is a fine and positive thing. But it can be done even while retaining a certain amount of competition. School prepares its pupils for life, and life has inequalities in it. Sport, which the young enjoy so much, is nothing but competition and emulation. A school without someone at the top and someone at the bottom is neither realistic nor attractive; it is too much like a flock of sheep.

Don Bosco saw love of the young in another way. 'I think,' he wrote, 'that it is a teacher's duty to bear in mind the least able in his class; to question them more than the others; to explain things to them for longer; to repeat and repeat until they have learnt, and to adapt homework and lessons to their capacity. To keep the brighter pupils busy, he should give them extra homework and lessons, and reward them with marks for diligence. Non-essential subjects should be given up, if teaching them means neglecting the slower children, and the main subjects must be treated in the way that suits them best.'

Perhaps you too would agree, Quintilian, that in the past the schools emphasized academic subjects too much. I can still remember the names of the Greek and Latin grammars and dictionaries we used, and linked to them are an endless string of declensions, rules, exceptions, exercises, and unseens.

History, the way I found it in school textbooks, seemed to me made up entirely of dates, wars, and peace treaties. In studying a little science, I learned by heart whole series of names like lepidoptera and coleoptera, whereas I was never sure which order the fly and the mosquito belonged to, nor was I ever able to recognize any of the orders in the red ants that nipped me painfully when I sat down in a field.

Today's living school is very much better. It offers children groups of interests. In language teaching it uses not just dictionaries but records and cassettes. In history it emphasizes the progress of culture and social conditions. In physics and the natural sciences it goes on the basis of laboratory experiments. And thus it accustoms children moderately to taking an interest and a part in the life and doings of their own surroundings and of the world in general.

I said 'moderately'. I'm sure that children can usefully discuss things in class, but I can't accept that they should fail to respect the teacher, swearing and making obscene gestures in his presence. I know that both the Italian Constitution and the Second Vatican Council recognized the right to strike; but I can't see this right vindicated in some of the schoolchildren's strikes, which end with stones thrown at the school windows and even worse sorts of vandalism.

* * *

During the next academic year, Law 477 will be applied to all Italian state schools—nursery, primary, secondary and technical schools—with important social results.

In Article 6 of this, parents are considered an integral and fundamental part of the school. A council will be set up, consisting of representatives of the teaching staff, the non-teaching staff, the pupils' parents and the headmaster, whether or not he teaches. It will be chaired by one of the parents, elected from among the members of the council. Parents will also form part of the pupils' disciplinary council and the class council.

This is a real advance, dear Quintilian. The parents thus officially become jointly responsible for the inner working of the school. But are they all prepared to deal with school problems? And will they manage to be guided only by their children's interests, and leave outside all matters of party, now that politics have seeped in everywhere, like a fine dust? Will the broad powers of deliberation allowed to parents in Article 6 not be cancelled out by the freedom to teach, which some teachers are already claiming, by appealing to Article 4? If teachers have too wide a freedom to teach what they feel like and what they think, then goodbye to the freedom of parents!

The Italian school faces a turnabout that will be historically important. If families don't understand it and don't keep their eyes open, it may turn out to be a disaster.

* * *

Illustrious Quintilian! Many centuries divide us. Many philosophers and many, many educators have come after you.

The humanistic culture, which was yours, is obscured today by knowledge of the world and of man; knowledge that, in this age of the atom and of technology, governs all. And yet a century ago Theodore Mommsen, a protestant Romanist, still called you 'inspired by good taste and proper judgement, instructive without pedantry'. Fifty years ago Concetto Marchesi, a communist, recognized your culture as being one that 'formed the spirit'.

I pray that not all humanistic culture will be lost in the schools and that your most famous maxims will continue to influence educators. The following one is enough: *Non multa, sed multum*; which can be translated into something like this: 'At school, don't learn many things, but learn what you do learn profoundly.'

Don Bosco used this in his own way when he wrote: 'The boy who does little does much, if he does what he should; and does little if he does much, but not what he ought to do.' Much, then, and deeply; without complicated exaggerations in the style of Anatole France.

He suggested that for an olive to be tasted to perfection, it should be put inside a lark, the lark put inside a pigeon, the pigeon into a chicken, the chicken in a guinea-pig, the guinea-pig in a calf, and the whole thing roasted on a spit. The best juices of the calf would therefore flow into those of the guinea-pig, which would flow into the chicken, the pigeon and the lark and finally into the olive, making it superlatively delicious. But no thank you! The price of that deliciousness is mass slaughter!

When you spoke of *multum*, Quintilian, you weren't thinking of a mass slaughter of values. Nor is that what we want in our schools.

GUGLIELMO MARCONI, Italian physicist (1874–1937), applied the electro-magnetic discoveries of Hertz and Maxwell to practical life, and produced the first means of long-distance radio communication through a long-wave circuit. After his early experiments in his home at Pontecchio he transmitted long-wave signals in 1895 and transatlantic signals in 1901. In 1909 he was awarded the Nobel Prize for Physics.

To Guglielmo Marconi

Illustrious Marconi,

We are celebrating the centenary of your birth (1874–1974). It was very fortunate for the world that, with your intellect, you concentrated from childhood on what fascinated you—the problems of modern physics.

At the age of twenty-one—without a degree, without even having finished your full time at secondary school—you had already discovered radio-telegraphy and were sending electric signals out across a distance. In the years that followed, new discoveries flooded out, one after another.

In 1924 you managed to perfect radio-phonics, making the human voice reach Australia from England. With the discovery of short waves and micro-waves you assured the new development of television.

I remember the interest with which the whole world followed you. I was just a poor boy, but I knew that in 1912, thanks to your invention, most of the passengers had been saved from the *Titanic* when it sank in a few hours after striking an iceberg. I heard people talk of your *Electra*, a laboratory ship, as if it were a ghost ship or something magical. It impressed me to see a photograph of you beside Pope Pius XI, to hear that at a mere signal from you thousands of lights had been switched on simultaneously in Sydney, and to know that you had crossed the Atlantic eighty-seven times for your experiments.

It looked as if things couldn't go further than that. Whereas?

Whereas we've continued to progress rapidly. If you now came back to the world, you'd find all kinds of new things since your death in 1937.

We now have colour television, video-cassettes, transistors, artificial satellites, radar, penicillin, reanimation chambers. In factories there are machines that produce objects by working on them from beginning to end without the components being touched by human hand. Other machines check products in such a way that faults are automatically detected and corrected. Electric brains register information and carry out the most varied tasks in the shortest time imaginable. Men have been to the moon and are planning to visit other planets. We are in the midst of the post-industrial, interplanetary, technological age.

* * *

Then all's well!—you'll say—since you were a successful entrepreneur and economist, as well as a great discoverer.

Let me make some distinctions. Many things *are* going well, but they're bringing us consequences that are full of problems and dangers. These will have to be corrected and channelled rather better.

Paul VI, for instance, has spoken of 'hungry peoples, who today are calling dramatically to the rich peoples', and of the 'anger of the poor, with its unforeseeable consequences'. This is what is happening: in a third of the world there is a remarkable abundance of everything and shameless waste; in two-thirds of the world there is poverty, which is steadily growing worse. If what is spent so easily on armaments was saved and certain luxuries were cut out, technology could soon take the whole human family to a fairly high level, economically, socially and culturally. This is well known and it is what angers the poor above all.

I spoke of the 'human family'. We have never felt, as we do today, how small the world is: we hunger and thirst for unity, but are continuously pulled between two opposing forces.

These things make for unity: the amazing network of communications that now binds the world in a hundred ways; the universal longing for peace; the existence of the United Nations Organization and other supranational organizations; the writings and the work of an élite of thinkers and politicians.

These make for disunity: the waves of exaggerated nationalism, which flare up every now and then here and there, in old peoples and in new ones; the division of the world into opposing blocks led by superpowers; social tensions, which are now no longer between classes but between regions and between rich states and poor states.

* * *

You'll also say: but I was a believer. Why doesn't the Church exploit the immense charge of renewal that is in the Gospel, renewing itself and moving on with the times?

Perfectly right. The Vatican Council has already used this idea in its message to thinkers and scientists. 'Your way,' it tells them, 'is ours. We are friends of your calling as researchers, we are allies of your efforts, admirers of your successes and, if need be, consolers of your discouragement and lack of success.' These are words I'm sure you'd have approved of, Marconi; and they're followed by deeds: an internal renewal is taking place within the Church and a dialogue is going on with the forces outside it.

But there are difficulties. As a bishop, I sometimes feel I'm in the shoes of the son of John II, King of France.

In 1356, at the Battle of Poitiers, the king was fighting fiercely. His son was fighting beside him, but he watched over his father and occasionally shouted: 'Father, look to the right! Father, look left!'

This is what I keep having to do. The Church wishes, for instance, to follow Rosmini's suggestion that we should 'listen to God worthily' through the right kind of liturgical celebration. This means stripping away the sometimes naive, exaggerated ways in which an agricultural, pre-scientific civilization regarded God.

But it's hard going. From the right, they shout that it's impiety and sacrilege every time an old rite is abandoned for a new one. On the left, it's the opposite: they want everything to be new for the sake of newness, are merrily dismantling the whole edifice of the past, putting statues and paintings in the attic, seeing idolatry and superstition everywhere, and even going so far as to say that for the sake of God's dignity we must speak of him in carefully chosen terms or even not mention him at all.

* * *

Illustrious Marconi! In the field of science, you rightly demanded physical and mathematical certainties. In other fields, you were content with the certainties of good sense and common sense. I know quite well that I can't speak of God in the way he deserves, but I must talk about him in some way.

I am like the mother who gave birth to a child in a prison without windows. The child grew up without ever having seen the sun. To give him an idea of it, when he was seven years old, she showed him a lantern the prison warder had lit. 'There,' she said, 'the sun is like that flame. It gives light and warmth, but is very, very much bigger.' It was very little, just an analogy, but it was better than nothing.

In the economic and social field, the Church is also finding it hard to make its contribution. As a Church, it says that it has no mandate or ability or means to solve strictly technical problems. The faithful, who are also citizens, must act in the world of trade unions, in politics, in business, inspired by their religious faith.

The hierarchy suggests that they and everyone else should take their social ideas from the principles of the Gospel, which today has to make its way between the opposing ideologies of capitalism and Marxism.

Capitalism deserves credit for promoting industrial development and defending personal freedom; but it can be reproached with having caused great suffering to the poor in the last century and many inequalities today.

Marxism tramples on personal freedom and sweeps away all religious values; but it cannot be denied credit for having opened many people's eyes to the sufferings of the workers and the duty of solidarity.

The Church teaches that capitalism must be changed profoundly. The riches it produces are good; but only so long as we do not become attached to them too much, so long as the greatest possible number of people have a share in them, and so long as it doesn't give rise to serious inequalities, such as we have today. Profit is good only if it is achieved with the right methods, that is, without sacrificing the dignity of a single human being. Even competition may be good, so long as it doesn't degenerate into a ferocious, pitiless struggle. The Church must love everyone, following the example of Jesus Christ, while preferring the poor and the least fortunate to all others.

As for Marxism, today it's trying to penetrate the Catholic ranks by making a subtle distinction. 'The analysis Marx made of society is one thing; the ideology that guided him is another. His analysis is strictly scientific and illuminating; it's useful for solving problems and we accept it. But the materialistic ideology we reject.'

The hierarchy is alarmed by this distinction. 'We refuse to accept the scientific character of an analysis which rests on a certain number of philosophical postulates, some arguable, some unacceptable,' the French bishops wrote on 14 November 1973.

Paul VI warned us (*Octuagesima Adveniens*, n. 34) that 'it would be illusory and dangerous . . . to accept the elements of Marxist analysis without recognizing their relationship with its ideology'.

Perhaps, dear Marconi, you will say to me: 'You are writing me a letter—a very humble literary form—which is quite inadequate as a criticism of the giants of capitalism and Marxism.' You're right, but what can I do? The fly kicks out where it can!

* * *

The Church's contribution to the unity of the world was expressed thus by Paul VI: 'The Church is expert in human matters . . . and without wishing to enter into politics . . . it offers what it has: a global vision of man and of humanity.' This vision has its roots in the Bible, which shows all men moving towards the same destiny, redeemed by a saviour, who is, and claims he is, on the side of the whole human race. This saviour's mission is 'to reconcile all things unto himself . . . whether they be things in earth, or things in heaven' (Col. 1, 20).

Jonah, in the Old Testament, didn't think he should have to share the privileges of his own people with others. When he was sent to preach at Nineveh, in the east, he tried, since the inhabitants of Nineveh weren't Jews, to flee westwards. God used a raging storm and the whale to send him back again.

When he preached to the Ninevites, Jonah hoped they wouldn't be converted. The opposite happened: they were converted, God forgave them, and Jonah, like a spoiled child, complained: 'I pray thee, O Lord, was not this my saying, when I was yet in my country? . . . for I knew that thou art a gracious God, and merciful, slow to anger, and of great kindness, and repenteth thee of the evil.'

But with a nice sense of humour, though quite firmly, God gave him a lesson in universalism.

Having left the city, Jonah made a shelter for himself against the heat and God gave him a hand. He 'prepared a gourd, and made it to come up over Jonah, that it might be a shadow over his head.' Jonah went to sleep happily, but in the morning found the plant withered and felt the sun burning down on his head. He lamented again, but God replied: 'Thou has had pity on the gourd, for the which thou hast not laboured, neither madest it grow; which came up in a night and perished in a night: And should I not spare Nineveh, that great city, wherein are more than six score thousand persons that cannot discern between their right hand and their left hand; and also much cattle.'

The theme of universalism—which is also very clear in the prophecies of Isaiah and Micah, and in some of the Psalms—is fully taken up by Jesus himself. At the crib, with the shepherds, come the non-Jewish Wise Men. The woman from Capernaum and the Roman centurion are also blessed and praised by him. The mission he gave to the Apostles was in these words: 'Go ye therefore, and teach all nations' (Matt. 28, 19); and St Paul could thus express the divine plan of salvation: 'And, having made peace through the blood of his cross, by him to reconcile all things unto himself; by him, I say, whether they be things in earth, or things in heaven' (Col. 1, 20).

In the same spirit, the last popes have warmly espoused the cause of unity and peace. Paul VI in particular tried using new methods—speaking to the United Nations Organization, and sending telegrams, offering his mediation, even to the heads of communist states.

You will say: and what was the result? At the very least, it made a widespread impression. People felt there was a new climate, and that changes were taking place. We are passing from what you might call the mentality of Gian Galeazzo Visconti to that of Petrarch.

Visconti, like the Renaissance prince he was, couldn't conceive of government without waging war, and even went so far as to forbid priests to say 'Give us peace' in the Mass.

Petrarch believed the exact opposite. He used to tell of a talk he once had with a madman. The madman saw some soldiers on the march and said to the poet: 'Where are they going?' 'To the wars,' said Petrarch. 'But,' said the madman, 'this war will have to end in peace some day, won't it?' 'Certainly,' said Petrarch. 'Well, then,' said the madman. 'Why not make peace at once, before starting the war?' 'I agree with that madman,' Petrarch said, in a melancholy way.

It would appear that a little of this beneficent madness is spreading to a number of people. And this is due, partly at least, to the Church.

* * *

Illustrious Marconi! The intense life you lived, entirely for research and for the development of your ideas, right up to the very last, can be summed up in these words: 'Few words, many deeds.' Teach us something of this, for today we seem to incline towards the opposite: we use many words (written or spoken) and produce very little from them.

GIUSEPPE GIOACCHINO BELLI, a poet who wrote in Roman dialect (1791–1863). During his best years as a writer (1830–36) he wrote two thousand sonnets. He is best known for his collection *I Sonetti Romaneschi*, in which he described with great candour the character, customs, faults and virtues of the Romans.

To Giuseppe Gioacchino Belli

Dear poet,

In your verses you treated my fellow-citizen from Belluno, Pope Gregory XVI, rather badly. But that doesn't prevent me seeing the quality of the more than two thousand sonnets in Roman dialect which you left us. Sometimes these depict the Roman people in the loveliest way—their language, temperament, customs and manners, their beliefs, prejudices, virtues and faults.

To tell the truth, you sometimes slipped down in your writing. You led the life of a gallant, and were determined to tell us so.

But what happy remarks you came out with! This, for instance: 'I don't say it to boast, but today's a most beautiful day'. Some of your sonnets are real *genre* paintings, from which artisans, working-class women, conspirators, shopkeepers, prelates and simple priests all leap out, wonderfully alive and seeming to speak to us.

One of your simple priests is the Abbot Francesco Cancellieri. You described him in some famous verses, and then went on in prose: Cancellieri, you said, 'started off talking of radishes, and from radishes went on to carrots, from carrots on to aubergines, and ended up with the burning of Troy!'

* * *

I'm sorry the good abbot gave conversation such a bad press, with his boring, inconclusive flood of talk. Because if it's carried on as it should be, it's really a very fine thing for poor souls like us.

Conversation brings us close to people and gives us a profound sense of ourselves. It relaxes us when we're tired, distracts us from our worries, develops our personality, and refreshes our thoughts.

Suppose I'm sad? The sympathy of the person I'm talking to

comforts me. Suppose I feel alone? Conversation cuts out loneliness. If it's friendly chat, then I'm happy to be allowed into the intimacy of others; if it's important talk, then I'm honoured to be treated as someone intelligent.

Is it the first time I've talked to someone? Then I feel I'm travelling pleasantly towards an unknown country. Is it the second, third or fourth time? I feel I'm returning to places I've already seen, the landscape and beauty of which I'm not yet familiar with. I find that when I'm talking to people I enrich myself, too. It's a fine thing to have firm convictions; but to have them in such a way that you can communicate them, and see them shared and appreciated, is even finer.

The clarity of things I've said increases the clarity of things I've thought. If I see that what I feel has had an effect on someone else's mind, then I feel it come back to me, shaken up and enlarged.

Jesus found relief in conversation, too. We have only to look at the confidences he gave his Apostles during the Last Supper to realize this. He often made conversation a vehicle for his apostolate; he would talk as he walked along the roads, or by the Temple; he talked in houses, with people around him, like Mary who sat at his feet, or John, who rested his head on his breast.

Several times I've wondered: why did Our Lord often express the highest truths while he was at the table? Perhaps because people put aside their worries during a meal and assume a calm, relaxed, unpretentious air. Worries and unpleasantness are small or don't exist at all at the table; people sit there feeling welcoming and sympathetic, not the least bit argumentative.

* * *

It was when we were talking at the table the day before yesterday, in fact, that I nearly managed to persuade a guest of mine. Between mouthfuls and smiles, he said that he was a firm supporter of pluralism in the faith. 'It's quite clear to me,' he said, 'that no one has the entire Christian truth in his pocket. Each of us has just a small piece of it and must be allowed to enjoy it in peace. Only God achieves unity from on high, putting together the various pieces and making a synthesis.' 'Oh dear,' I said. 'Forgive me for saying it, but your idea of God and truth seems to me like that of the Indian blind men.' 'What blind men?' he said. 'Wait,' I said, and got up.

I left the room and came back with one of Leo Tolstoy's books. 'Let me read you just one page,' I said, and read *The King's Elephant*, a fable.

An Indian king ordered all blind men that could be found to be rounded up, and when this was done he had them shown his elephant. One of them patted a leg, another the tail, a third the beginning of the tail, a fourth the belly, a fifth the back, a sixth the ears, a seventh the teeth and an eighth the trunk.

Then the king had all the blind men brought before him and said: 'What is my elephant like?'

The first blind man said: 'Your elephant is like pillars.' He was the one who'd patted its legs. The second said it was like

a broom. He was the one who'd touched its tail. The third said it was like a branch. He was the one who'd touched the top of the tail. The one who'd touched the stomach said: 'Your elephant's like a pile of earth.' The one who'd touched the sides said: 'It's like a wall.' The one who'd touched the back said: 'It's like a mountain.' The one who'd touched the ears said: 'It's like a battering ram.' The one who'd touched the tusks said: 'It's like horns.' The one who'd touched the trunk said: 'It's like thick rope.' And all the blind men began quarrelling and arguing among themselves.

I put down the book and said: 'Listen. I hate to think that God sent his son to say: "I am the way, the truth and the light," and that we're now like those blind men, each of us holding a tiny part of the truth, and each part different from the others. It's true that we know the truths of faith only through analogy, but we're not as blind as all that! It seems to me unworthy both of God and of our own reasoning.'

This unexpected theological argument, based on the elephant's tail, back and trunk, didn't persuade my guest entirely, but it shook him. 'Well!' he said. 'No one ever said that to me!' 'It's sometimes the goslings that show the geese where to drink,' I told him. Where Rahner doesn't succeed with his great tomes of theology, Tolstoy may creep in with his fables.

* * *

From Rahner to Tolstoy, dear Belli, I get back to you, realizing that there's the other side of the coin in conversation. Your Cancellieri's verbosity is only one of a great many defects. Goldini described the trouble caused by women's gossip, and by lies—which his character Lelio calls 'witty inventions'; and by women who ask their friends to keep secrets purely in order to have them spread about.

We should never talk at the expense of charity, truth, our work, and our study; in other words we should look for moderation in our talk.

* * *

Conversation is quite different from chatter. Chat strings pointless bits of news together, hides our minds instead of revealing them, cuts out other speakers, deafens people, and leaves them feeling limp.

I've read that when he was travelling in Holland Thomas More met a man on the road who spoke very agreeably, left the person he was talking to room to talk as well, and was delightful both in what he said and in the lively way he said it. More admired his conversation so much that, after a particularly witty remark, he exclaimed: 'Well, you must be either the Devil or else Erasmus of Rotterdam.' 'I'm not the Devil,' answered his companion. 'But I am Erasmus.'

This story shows that conversation reveals us as we are, and that we should try and say useful, interesting, pleasing things, without scolding or posing, without choosing our words too carefully or using high-sounding ones. High-sounding words, dear Belli, were things you didn't like either, as you said quite clearly.

If you came back today, you'd find all sorts of high-sounding cliches; people talk of 'facing up to the word of God', 'prophetic speeches and gestures', 'mediation between faith and history', 'structuralism', 'liberation', 'verification', 'reading so-and-so in the field of such-and-such', 'being on the level of this-that-or-the-other'. All these words express important ideas, of course, but it's rather funny to see people who call themselves non-conformists 'conforming' merrily to these words just because they're used by important people. Other phrases surprise me, as some surprised you. You couldn't understand why they were used in your day, and I'm not able to understand now. Can it be the fault of fashion? That's been defined as 'a horror of the immediate past', 'not the mother of good sense, but its mother-in-law, its tyrant'.

How much better if, at least in conversation, instead of using hard, fashionable words we used easy simple ones—maybe borrowed from Tolstoy's fables or (obviously well chosen and well purged!) from your sonnets.

Félix Dupanloup, Bishop of Orléans, was born at St Félix in the Savoy in 1802 and died at Lacombe in 1878. He is best known for his tireless zeal in the education of the clergy and young people, and in the teaching of the catechism. He wrote on education, fought for the freedom of teaching, and was active in French politics.

To Félix Dupanloup

Dear Bishop and Academician of France,

'A burning coal over which nature sometimes blew, and sometimes grace.' Thus were you described. I find that grace 'blew' in you much more than nature.

Even when you were fighting your great battles in the newspapers or in the French National Assembly, in the senate or in the First Vatican Council, you were always guided and animated by a profound religious feeling; and by a heart that was enthusiastic, but loyal and upright.

You were head of a seminary, and even Renan, who was an ex-pupil of yours, said you were 'unequalled as an educator'.

There was a campaign for free schooling, and Lacordaire, Montalembert and Falloux had you on their side in the struggle and the victory.

Pius IX's *Syllabus* appeared, arousing loud, distressing reactions; and you made a comment on it so moderate and wise that the storm was partly calmed, at least six hundred bishops applauded, and Pius IX himself approved.

Everyone thought that Talleyrand, that great sinner and apostate, was irretrievably lost. God recovered him, but used you to do it—your tact, your understanding and your patience.

In other words, you were a great bishop, a great literary man, and a central figure in all the movements of ideas and opinions in your century.

But to me the most interesting thing about you and your work is your passion for the catechism.

You began to instruct small children while you were still a choirboy at San Sulpice. You continued as a very young priest at the Assumption and the Madeleine. All Paris came to hear you. When you became a bishop the catechism was still your main interest and filled most of your books. In your diary you wrote: 'As soon as I was given a class of small children I took fire. From then on, what was not the catechism—that is, the pure action of

245

grace upon souls—became of no importance to me. The unimportant literary man who was a part of me gave way entirely to the catechist.' You also wrote: 'The finest of all ministries is that of the pastoral minister. But the catechism is even finer. It is the ideal in God's heart. Nothing can be compared with it. It is the purest ministry, the most disinterested, and the most unpretentious.'

* * *

I'm reminded of you particularly, and of these passionate convictions of yours, because I've been looking at the text of the children's catechism that will be tried out in Italy from next October. It's a good text, I think. But what's the good of the text if we don't possess the hearts and minds of those who will teach it?

When I was a young priest I was told: 'The text is a help, a stimulus; not a comfortable armchair in which the teacher settles down for a rest.' 'The text, however good, is dead: it's the catechist's business to bring it alive.' 'The lesson is only as good as the homework before it.' 'In teaching young children you teach them not so much what you know as what you are. Fine words from the teacher aren't much good if his behaviour speaks in another way and proves them wrong.'

I was also told about Pedro Ribadeneira, a lively lad brought to Rome from Spain by St Ignatius. 'Make the sign of the cross more correctly,' St Ignatius told him one day. 'Father, I make it just like your Jesuits,' said the boy. 'Whatever do you mean? My Jesuits make the sign of the cross exactly as they should,' said Ignatius.

The boy said nothing, but thought his own thoughts.

In the morning the Jesuits got up very early and, in their dark clothes and white cottas, went along the dark corridors to the chapel. Pedro filled the holy water stoups with ink, and as the Jesuits passed they dipped their fingers into them and made the sign of the cross. Then they went to their seats to meditate, and when it was over put their cottas in the sacristy. Pedro quickly bundled these up and took them along to St Ignatius. 'Father,' he said, 'come and check your dear Jesuits' signs of the cross.' Alas, the ink spots said clearly that Jesuits sometimes make the sign of the cross as carelessly as anyone else.

And here, in my imagination, I see all the lay catechists. Parents first of all. They are, the Council said, 'the first preachers of the word'. Religious statues about the house, prayers said at home, the parents' conversation and their respect for priests and for everything connected with religion, all make children feel warm and comfortable in a religious atmosphere. But much more is needed.

Windhorst, a German statesman, asked by a lady how she should pose for a photographer, replied: 'Holding your catechism, madam, as you teach it to your children.'

The first religious book children read is the parents themselves. If a father says to his son: 'A monk's hearing confessions in church, why not go along?', it's a good thing. But it's a better thing if he says: 'I'm off to church to go to confession. Like to come along too?'

* * *

But I meet objectors sometimes today: parents who call themselves Christians, but actually put off having their children baptized. 'No pressure's going to be put on my child,' they say. 'He'll choose when he's twenty or so.' Dear Dupanloup, you've answered this objection already: 'At twenty!' you said. 'The age at which, more than at any other, your child will need a faith that has penetrated into the innermost parts of his being! And how will a twenty-year-old choose between the many religions that exist unless he's studied them all first? And how can he possibly study them all, being completely taken up with school and sport and fun and friendships? If we are to inherit a fortune, all we need to do is to be born. Inheriting a fortune is good luck, and even if a child doesn't realize it, he'll be very pleased with his fortune when the time comes, and very well aware of it. Now, if a father is a serious Christian, he must think that becoming a child of God and a brother of Christ through baptism is an immense piece of good fortune. Why should he deprive his child of it?'

'Yes,' says the objector, 'but this good fortune involves heavy moral commitments. My child shouldn't be landed with them without being asked.'

Dear Dupanloup, you've answered this one too. How many things are imposed on children without their permission? You've brought them into the world without a 'by your leave'. Name, family, surroundings, social position, clothes, and school are all imposed on the child in those early years without his permission being asked. And anyway, is it a misfortune for your child to have good Christian laws to obey? Did God give men his laws just for a whim, for some trivial purpose or advantage of his own? Doesn't the acceptance of duties and limitations make man great and happy? And what about freedom? Well, this doesn't consist in doing whatever you like but in doing what you should!

* * *

After the parents, the next catechists are the child's primary school teachers. You wrote some fine things about your first teachers.

I think with tenderness of mine, and share Otto Ernst's opinion: 'I think there is nothing finer than a primary school teacher,' he wrote. I can see myself as a child on the school bench at Canale, feeling as Goldsmith's schoolchildren did in *The Deserted Village*:

'While words of learned length and thundering sound
Amazed the gazing rustics ranged around;
And still they gazed, and still the wonder grew,
That one small head could carry all he knew.'

Let me make myself clear, I'm not so ingenuous as to make myths out of children and their teachers. There's also the reverse of the coin, I know. Children are as innocent as angels, but often as proud as princes, as bold as heroes, as uncontrolled as colts, as obstinate as donkeys, as changeable as sunflowers, with throats as long as the necks of cranes; but always at a marvellous, confident, malleable age.

Then there are the teachers. Some of them realize that

children need a leader, someone who makes an impression on them by being clever and likeable. Some, though, are tamed instead of being tamers.

The tamed teacher is like the mistress of the youngest class, recalled by our Mosca. As he walked down the passage, he heard her voice. 'Have horses got fifteen legs?' he heard her ask. 'No,' the children answered in chorus. 'Have they twelve?' 'No!' And so she went on, down all the possible number of legs until she came to the right number. 'Have they four?' 'No!' the children chanted merrily. Poor silly teacher!

Mosca himself was quite different. How did he come to tame the terrible Form 5C? It was simple: by making his forty children like him. But how did he make them like him? 'A big fly was my salvation,' he tells us.

A fly came into the classroom and distracted all the children with its buzzing. Another master might have said 'Listen to me and not the fly!' But Mosca said to one of the children: 'Think you could give that fly a whack?' 'Leave it to me,' said the boy, and climbed up on to the bench. There he aimed at the fly but missed. 'Let me have a go,' said Mosca, aiming at the fly. This time it was caught and fell dead at Mosca's feet. Now that was really clever, and brought all those defiant, threatening children over to his side.

'If you had a moustache, at least,' the headmaster said to Mosca, feeling uneasy because he looked so young. There are things more important than moustaches, though, as you can see. The good a master can do in teaching religion to children is incalculable.

On one condition, though: that he teaches the authentic word of God faithfully, and not his own personal opinion. Sometimes this happens: progress is mistaken for truth and what the Church's teachers say is despised. New things must be substituted for old, it's said. If it's a case of secondary, outgrown aspects of the Church, this may be perfectly right, even necessary, but in other cases it may be very dangerous.

Teachers tell their pupils the story of Aladdin and the wonderful lamp he got away from the magician. The magician wants revenge on Aladdin and goes through the streets shouting: 'New lamps for old! New lamps for old!' It seems a bargain, but in fact it's a trick. Aladdin's credulous wife falls for it. As her husband is away, she goes up to the attic and gets the lamp—knowing nothing about its powers—and gives it to the magician. He carries it off, leaving some valueless shiny tin lamps in exchange.

This trick is still used: every now and then a magician comes along—mystical, philosophical, or political—who offers to trade his goods. Be careful. Some magicians offer glittering ideas which may be tinny rather than solid, human, transitory, fashionable things. What are called old outmoded ideas are often the ideas of God, of which it is written: 'not a jot or tittle shall pass away . . .'

Dear Dupanloup, in writing all this about catechism and teachers I've forgotten you.

But you had something to say to them. And that is: unite loyalty to God with faith in the true values of modern civilization, and in the perpetual youthfulness of the Church.

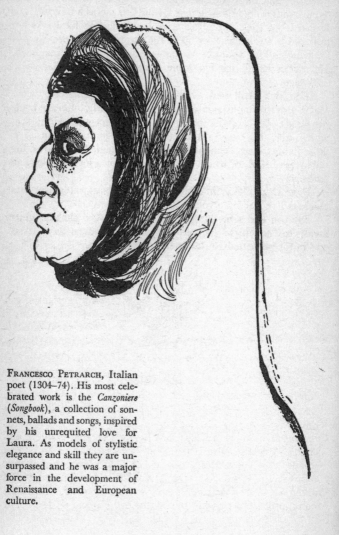

FRANCESCO PETRARCH, Italian
poet (1304–74). His most celebrated work is the *Canzoniere*
(*Songbook*), a collection of sonnets, ballads and songs, inspired
by his unrequited love for
Laura. As models of stylistic
elegance and skill they are un-
surpassed and he was a major
force in the development of
Renaissance and European
culture.

To Petrarch

Illustrious poet,

In Italy and outside it, the six hundredth anniversary of your death is being celebrated this year (1374–1974).

Congresses, studies and publications of all kinds are dealing with you, with this or that aspect of your personality and your immense literary output.

Although you have been dead for so long, you appear more alive than ever. As a man of letters, as a very subtle psychologist, as a political animal, as a dedicated tourist, as a sincere and at the same time a critical Christian, and as a hundred other things, you continue to arouse interest and curiosity today.

Will anyone speak of you as a repentant but backsliding sinner, a Christian often thirsting for sanctity yet unable to make a complete break with sin and to renounce the passions, great and small, that you loved? I don't know. But if anyone does, he will have to deal with your attitude to confession.

Because, dear Petrarch, you used to go to confession.

Writing from Rome to your friend Giovanni Boccaccio, you told him of the misfortune that had befallen you: a bad kick on your knee from a shod horse had given you a fortnight of acute pain: 'I accept it all as a punishment for my sins,' you wrote, 'and in exchange for the penance which my too-kind confessor failed to give me.'

The effort you put into examining the very depths of your soul appears in your books; as when you wrote that you were too pleased with your own mind and eloquence, with the culture you had acquired and even with your own appearance; or when you reproached yourself for longing for honours, comfort and riches, and for having all too often given way to lust. You groaned over the chains of passion which you couldn't manage to break, of the force of 'perverse habits', of the 'bitter taste' of falling yet again into sin. Writing to your brother, who was a monk, you deplored your 'desire for very elegant clothes,' your 'fear that a hat would be blown away and a light wind would blow about the careful arrangement of [your] hair'. The curling pins you put in your hair at night broke your sleep and inflicted worse pain than that of 'a cruel pirate', but you wouldn't hear of giving them up. And in an imaginary conversation with St Augustine, you posed some disquieting questions. '*Falling* was my fault, but *lying* there, not getting up, does not depend on me,' you said. 'It depends partly on you,' said St Augustine. 'But you can see that I weep over my own wretchedness,' you replied. 'It's not a matter of weeping,' said Augustine, 'but of willing.'

Fortunately, you were never without the right principle: God can save me, in spite of my own weakness. God's mercy avoids fears, and solves many problems.

* * *

At a distance of six hundred years, are we, today's penitents, better or worse than you were? This is a question that makes me wonder.

It seems to me that we are less ready to recognize our own weaknesses. We often say: 'Holy Mary . . . pray for us sinners', 'Father . . . forgive us our trespasses', 'Lamb of God . . . have mercy on us', but very superficially. In practice we justify ourselves with the strangest excuses ('we are free, autonomous, mature'); we appeal to the demands of nature, instinct, culture and fashion. In the Book of Proverbs we are told: 'Such is the way of an adulterous woman; she eateth, and wipeth her mouth, and saith, I have done no wickedness.' This woman, dear Petrarch, is an emblematic figure; she shows exactly what much of our permissive Christian civilisation is like.

We are not short of tears, as you were not: what we lack is the will: or rather, we often dislike what we liked when we were sinning, and disapprove of what we once approved, but we don't get down to what is more practical: fleeing from occasions of sin. You who carried the *Confessions* of St Augustine, even when you climbed up Mount Ventoux, had the case of Alypius as an example.

A strong man, able to stand up to the most powerful senators, he had come to Rome from Africa and was 'utterly averse to and detested' the gladiatorial fights in which one man killed another for the entertainment of others. Friends suggested he should watch a fight, and although at first Alypius refused he later agreed. 'Though you hale my body to that place,' he said: 'and there set me, can you force me also to turn my mind or my eyes to those shows? I shall then be absent while present, and so shall overcome both you and them.' Alas, a great roar from the audience made him open his eyes. Then he 'was stricken with a deeper wound in his soul, than the other, who he desired to behold, was in his body; and he fell more miserably than he, upon whose fall that mighty noise was raised, which entered through his ears, and unlocked his eyes to make way for the striking and beating down of a soul, bold rather than resolute, and the weaker in that it had presumed on itself, which ought to have relied on thee. For so soon as he saw that blood, he therewith drunk down savageness; nor turned away, but fixed his eye, drinking in frenzy, unawares, and was delighted with that guilty fight, and intoxicated with the bloody pastime. Nor was he now the man he came, but one of the throng he came unto, yea, a true associate of theirs that had brought him thither. Why say more? He beheld, shouted, kindled, carried thence with him the madness which should goad him to return not only with them who first drew him thither, but also before them, yea and to draw in others. Yet thence did thou with a most strong and most merciful hand pluck him, and taughtest him to have confidence not in himself, but in thee. But this was after.' (*Confessions*, Book VI.)

Unfortunately we all share the amazing weakness of Alypius (who was later a bishop and a saint). For this reason, in every confession, we are urged to pray: 'I propose ... to flee from the occasions of sin.'

I fear we are more incomplete than you, dear Petrarch, as far as trust in God is concerned. God is the father of the prodigal son, we agree; Jesus is the good shepherd, who takes the frightened lamb back to the flock, who pardoned the adulterous woman, Zacchaeus, and the Good Thief. Everyone goes that far, or nearly everyone.

But some say 'I will deal directly with God', and don't follow you into the confessional. The confessor mediates between God and the sinner; for Jesus said to the Apostles: 'Whose sins you shall forgive, they are forgiven.'

These people don't realize that the confessor doesn't just *declare* forgiveness for past sins but *grants* forgiveness and hands out a sentence.

And this sentence can't be left to a pure whim of the priest ('I like you, so I'll absolve you'). It must be based on closely examined elements that are absolutely certain; and these, only the penitent can provide—by making his confession, in fact.

* * *

You found your confessor 'too kind'. In our day, those who go to confession look for confessors who are kind but not 'too kind'. Auguste Conte, an eminent philosopher, dedicated an entire chapter full of affectionate gratitude to his confessors, in his book *The Awakening of the Soul*.

St Jeanne Chantal and other penitents were very happy with St Francis de Sales, who was both father and physician in the confessional, and above all able to fill them with courage. 'Holiness,' he said, 'consists in fighting faults. But how can we fight them if they aren't there? How can we overcome them if we don't meet them? Being wounded occasionally in battle doesn't mean being vanquished. Only someone who loses life or courage is vanquished. Anyone who decides to carry on fighting is a victor.'

That's the kind of confessor people expect today: firm, but delicate; a lover of God, but one who knows the problems of men.

Today, though, the Church wants emphasis laid not so much on the sins the penitent has accused himself of, as upon conversion, seen biblically not just as a way of getting away from sin but also—and much more—as an approach to God and a loving embrace with him. 'Let yourselves be reconciled with God,' St Paul said. We repeat this today and hope that reconciliation is preceded by the word of God himself, read and meditated upon. In fact, we go to God, if he first calls us and speaks to us. We also hope that this word may possibly come to us not individually, but joined together in a community.

In the Middle Ages, dear Petrarch, you people made confession something very personal and secret. Today people look back nostalgically to the old days, when, at the end of Lent, the bishop gave his hand to the first of the penitents, who gave his to the next, until all were joined in a long chain and brought into the Church for a solemn reconciliation.

* * *

How often you went to confession, I don't know.

In the Middle Ages, people went to confession a lot and to communion very little. Today, the opposite seems to happen: even pious souls are slightly allergic to frequent confessions and devotions.

These people make me think of Jonathan Swift's servant. After spending the night at an inn, Swift asked for his boots in the morning and saw them brought in covered in dust. 'Why didn't you clean them?' he asked. 'I thought there was no point,' said the servant. 'After a few miles on the road, they'll be covered in dust again, whatever I do.' 'Quite right, now go and get the horses ready; we're leaving.' Soon afterwards the horses came out of the stable and Swift was ready for the journey. 'But we can't leave without breakfast!' cried his servant. 'There's no point,' replied Swift. 'After a few miles on the road you'll be hungry again!'

* * *

Dear Petrarch, neither you nor I follow the logic of Swift's servant, do we? After confession the soul will grow dirty again, people say. Very likely. But to keep it clean in the meantime can't fail to be a good idea. Not only because confession takes away the dust of sin, but because it gives us a special strength to avoid it, and makes firmer our friendship with God.

St Theresa of Avila, a Spanish Carmelite nun originally called Teresa de Ceñeda y Ahumada (1515–82). She came from a rich, noble family in Avila, and became a Carmelite nun at the age of twenty-one, and set about vigorously reforming her order, which she wished to restore to its original austerity. Her writings, in simple, straightforward language are some of the greatest in mystical literature and include *The Way of Perfection*, an Autobiography and Letters.

To St Theresa of Avila

Dear St Theresa,

As your feast day falls in October, I thought you might allow me to write you a letter this month.

Anyone who looks at Bernini's famous marble group, in which he depicts you pierced by the seraph's arrow, will think of your visions and ecstasies. And rightly so: the mystical Theresa, rapt away in God, is a true Theresa.

But there's another Theresa, one I like better: the one who is close to us and who emerges from the *Autobiography* and from the *Letters*. This is the Theresa of everyday life, who feels the same difficulties as we do and can skilfully surmount them; who can smile and laugh and make others laugh; who moved about the world with great self-possession and lived through the most varied events, helped by her many natural gifts but even more by her constant union with God.

The Protestant reformation broke out, and the situation of the Church in Germany and France was critical. It saddened you, Theresa. 'If I could have saved a single soul among the many lost there, I would have sacrificed my life a thousand times,' you said. 'But I was a woman!'

A woman! But one worth twenty men, who left no method untried and managed to carry out splendid internal reforms and influence the whole Church with her work and writings; the first, and—with St Catherine—the only woman to be proclaimed a Doctor of the Church.

You were a woman who spoke out frankly, dear Theresa, and wrote in a polished, cutting style. Although you had a very elevated idea of the mission of nuns, you wrote to Father Graziano: 'For the love of God, be careful what you do! Never believe nuns, because if they want something they'll try every possible means to get it.' And to Father Ambrose, refusing a postulant, you said: 'You make me laugh when you say you

259

know her soul just by seeing her. It's not so easy to know women!'

Yours was the perfect definition of the devil: 'That poor wretch, who cannot love.'

To Don Sancho Davila you wrote: 'I have distractions too, in reciting the divine office. I confessed it to Father Dominic, who told me to take no notice. I say the same to you, because it's an incurable disease.' This was spiritual advice, but you were very free with advice of all kinds. You even advised Father Graziano to make his journeys on a better-tempered donkey, one without the bad habit of tossing friars to the ground; or else to have himself tied to the donkey to avoid tumbling off.

But when the time came to do battle, you seemed unconquerable. The papal nuncio, no less, had you shut up in the convent in Toledo, declaring you to be 'an unquiet, wandering, disobedient, and quarrelsome woman'. But from your convent the messages you sent to Philip II, and to princes and prelates, sorted everything out.

Your conclusion was this: 'Theresa on her own is worth nothing; Theresa and a penny are worth less than nothing; Theresa, a penny and God can do everything!'

* * *

To me, you are a remarkable example of something that keeps turning up regularly in the Catholic Church.

Women don't rule in the Church—that's a function of the hierarchy—but very often they inspire, promote and sometimes direct.

On the one hand the spirit 'blows where it will'; on the other, women are more sensitive to religion than men and more capable of giving themselves generously to great causes. This means that a great many women saints, mystics and foundresses have been found in the Catholic Church. There are also women who led religious movements, and influenced a very wide range of people.

Marcella, a noblewoman who directed a kind of convent of rich and cultivated patricians on the Aventine, collaborated

with St Jerome in translating the Bible.

At the beginning of the seventeenth century Madame Acarie influenced distinguished people such as the Jesuit Coton, Friar Canflet, St Francis de Sales and many others, and thus had an effect upon the whole of French spirituality at the time.

Princess Amalia Gallitzin, who was appreciated even by Goethe, from the 'Munster circle' spread a current of intensely spiritual life through the whole of northern Germany. Sophia Swetchine, a Russian convert in the early nineteenth century, turned up in France and became the 'spiritual directress' of all kinds of people, lay and clerical.

I could cite other examples, but I will come back to you, Theresa, who were not so much the daughter as the spiritual mother of St John of the Cross and the first reformed Carmelites. Today there are no problems in the Carmelite Order, but in your day there was the row I mentioned earlier.

You were on one side, full of charismatic gifts, and of ardent, luminous strength given to you for the benefit of Church; on the other stood the papal nuncio, or rather the hierarchy which had to judge the authenticity of your gifts. At first, on the basis of distorted information, the nuncio decided against you. Once he had had things explained to him and had examined them better, everything was cleared up, the hierarchy approved, and your gifts were able to expand in the service of the Church.

* * *

Today, we also hear a great deal about charismatic gifts and the hierarchy. Although you were a specialist in these matters, allow me to take the following principles from your works.

1) The Holy Spirit is above everything. Both the charismatic gifts and the powers of our pastors come from him. He sees to it that there is harmony and agreement between the hierarchy and the charismatics, and thus ensures the unity of the Church.

2) Charismatics and the hierarchy are both necessary to the Church, but in different ways. The charismatics act as accelerators, favouring progress and renewal. The hierarchy must use the brake, in favour of stability and prudence.

3) Charismatics and the hierarchy sometimes cut across each other and overlap. Certain charismatics in fact are given to the pastors mainly as the 'gifts' mentioned by St Paul in the First Epistle to the Corinthians. On the other hand, since the hierarchy has to regulate all the main stages of ecclesiastical life, charismatics cannot, with the excuse that they have visions, remove themselves from its guidance.

4) Charismatic experiences are not anyone's private reserve. They may be given to anyone: priests and laymen, men and women. It is one thing, though, to be *able* to have visions, and quite another actually to *have* them. In your *Libro de las fundaciones* I find written: 'A woman penitent told her confessor that the Madonna often came to see her and stayed talking to her for over an hour, revealing the future and many other things to her. And as something true occasionally emerged from all the nonsense, it all seemed to be true. I realized at once what it was all about ... but I merely told the confessor to wait for the result of these prophecies, to find out for himself about the penitent's way of life and to look for further signs of sanctity in her. In the end ... it was seen that her visions were all fantasies.'

* * *

Dear St Theresa, if only you could come back today! The word 'charisma' is squandered. All kinds of people are known as 'prophets', even the students who confront the police in the streets, or the guerrillas of Latin America. People try to set up the charismatics in opposition to the pastors. What would you say?—you who obeyed your confessors, even when their advice turned out to be the opposite of that given to you by God in prayer?

Don't think I'm a pessimist. I hope this business of seeing visions everywhere is just a bad habit that will pass. On the other hand I know that the authentic gifts of the Spirit are always accompanied by abuses and false gifts. And the Church has gone on just the same.

In the young Church of Corinth, for instance, visionaries

flourished. But St Paul was rather worried about it because he'd found some abuses. Later these abuses became more noticeably aberrant.

Two women, Priscilla and Massimilia, who supported and financed Montanism in Asia, began by preaching a moral awakening 'charismatically'; this involved great austerity, the total renunciation of marriage, and absolute readiness for martyrdom. They ended by setting up new prophets against the bishops. These men and women, 'filled with the spirit', preached, administered the sacraments, and waited for Christ, who was to come and inaugurate the new kingdom of heaven at any moment.

In the time of St Augustine we find Lucilla of Carthage, a rich lady whom Bishop Ceciliano had scolded because she used to press a small bone of some martyr to her breast before communion. Hurt and angry, Lucilla induced a group of bishops to oppose Ceciliano. They failed to establish their point in Africa, but protested successfully to the Pope, then to the Council at Arles, finally to the Emperor himself. A new Church began. In nearly all the cities of Africa there were thus two bishops, and two cathedrals frequented by two opposing categories of the faithful, who, when they met, came to blows. Catholics on the one hand; the followers of Donato and Lucilla on the other.

Donato's followers called themselves 'the Pure'. They never sat down in a place previously occupied by a Catholic without first cleaning it with their sleeve. They avoided the Catholic bishops like the plague, appealed to the Gospel against the Church, which they said was supported by the authority of the Emperor, and set up assault squads. One day the mild St Augustine said: 'If you want martyrdom so much, why don't you take a rope and hang yourselves?'

In the seventeenth century, there were the nuns of Port Royal. One of their abbesses, Mother Angelica, had started well: she had 'charismatically' reformed herself and the monastery, keeping even parents out of the cloister. She had great gifts and was born to rule, but she became the soul of Jansenist resistance, intransigent to the last in the face of the ecclesiastical authorities.

Of her and of her nuns it was said that they were 'as pure as angels and as proud as devils'.

How far all this is from your spirit, Theresa! What a gulf between these women and you! 'Daughter of the Church' was the name you loved best. You murmured it on your deathbed; while in life you worked hard *for* the Church and *with* the Church, even accepting a certain amount of suffering *from* the Church. Couldn't you teach some of today's 'prophetesses' a little of your method?

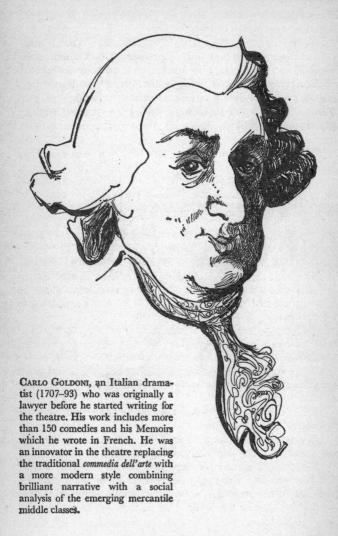

CARLO GOLDONI, an Italian dramatist (1707–93) who was originally a
lawyer before he started writing for
the theatre. His work includes more
than 150 comedies and his Memoirs
which he wrote in French. He was
an innovator in the theatre replacing
the traditional *commedia dell'arte* with
a more modern style combining
brilliant narrative with a social
analysis of the emerging mercantile
middle classes.

To Carlo Goldoni

Dear Goldoni,

At the end of August this year, 1974, I had the chance of seeing your *Rusteghi*, and some time ago I saw Shakespeare's *Taming of the Shrew*. Quite spontaneously I found myself thinking of the contrast between the anti-feminist Shakespeare and you, the feminist.

The shrew is Katherine, daughter of a rich man in Padua. Haughty, cross-grained, refusing to put up with anyone or anything, she flings the furniture about, chases people out of the house, and even has the charming habit of biting. So nobody wants to marry her.

Petruccio arrives from Verona, covets Katherine's dowry, and asks for her hand. She spurns him, but the cunning, unflappable Petruccio continues his clever courtship. The nastier she is to him, the more he claims to find her sweet and kind.

They get married, and Petruccio takes Katherine to Verona, where their roles are reversed. He claims that the food and the bed aren't worthy of her, and, while professing to love her dearly, denies her food and sleep.

Without either, Katherine is tamed. When her husband tells her to do so she is ready to call the sun the moon and vice versa, or to say it's fine when it's raining. She tells her father, sister, brother-in-law and the audience that a woman's duty is to obey and serve her husband and to agree with him in everything.

In *I Rusteghi*, the opposite happens: four husbands start off as 'tamers' and end up 'tamed'.

And what about their wives? The attitude was: 'Let her stay at home, seeing nobody, meeting nobody.'

What about Lunardo's daughter, one of the four wives? On her wedding day she doesn't even know she's engaged and has never seen the man. The whole thing has been arranged in great secrecy by the fathers of the bride and groom. The bride complains to her stepmother that she's never allowed out of doors.

Then the wives go into the attack, led by the enterprising Felice who, having discovered the secret of the coming wedding and given the men a big surprise, overcomes their final resistance with a speech worthy of a lawyer, which leaves them stunned.

The four men, overwhelmed rather than persuaded, have to agree that wives and daughters shouldn't be tamed but should be listened to. In any case, whether the husbands agree or not, the wives are going to be heard.

* * *

When I consider your play and Shakespeare's, dear Goldoni, I prefer yours. It's more human, fairer, closer to the reality of those days and of today, even if your feminism now looks rather pale. Women have come a long way, after all, since then! Which is quite right, on the whole. In *Le femmine puntigliose*, you laughed at ladies in their drawing rooms. Well, today all you laughed at has vanished. And another thing that's almost entirely vanished is the difference between 'ladies' and working-class women.

Time, and in particular the two terrible wars, with the way they mixed up so many things in life, have changed the outlook and social position of women. Girls are no longer shut up at home. Even the richest study and prepare themselves for a job with which to earn their living. Men may still bow to them and kiss their hands, but rather hurriedly. They know that in general they've got to rely on themselves, they've got to be self-sufficient, like men, and contribute like them to the family finances.

As in your day, Goldoni, women have great intuitive powers, a great capacity for feeling; but today they've got to use half for the family and the other half to build up a social position and maintain it.

In your plays, women can be divided into categories that are counted on the fingers of one hand: noblewoman, bourgeois lady, working-class woman, innkeeper, servant. Today it would take a whole dictionary to list them: shop girls, students, window dressers, schoolteachers, air hostesses, nurses, secretaries, doctors, policewomen, social workers, lawyers; and so on, endlessly, up to members of parliament and ministers in the government.

'She can do everything,' you make Lunardo say about his daughter Lucietta. And what you mean is: knitting, mending, embroidery, cooking, music.

Today, a women's work may be anything at all. She may do things that in your day, dear Goldoni, were a man's preserve. Today you find women in politics and sport, often showing a tough, free-and-easy attitude, disdaining or pretending to disdain any external show of feeling. Inwardly, perhaps, they may dream and weep as the girls in your plays do; but outwardly they show, for the most part, a mask of indifference.

* * *

At this point you'll ask: 'But do you think all this is good or bad?' In itself it's good, dear Goldoni. The bad, if there is any, lies in the deterioration of the atmosphere in which the women are living today and which influences their healthy convictions and their religious and moral life. On July 26th, for instance, an Italian daily paper wrote: 'Yesterday, at a press conference, the woman Deputy N., proposing the liberalization of the abortion laws, declared: "The right to live our own sexuality is limited today by the sense of sin . . . A woman has a right to live her own sexuality not only within the context of a family and with a family in mind."'

Dear Goldoni, you weren't what's called a bigot, you spoke little of God and even treated some clerics with a touch of irony. You were a lawyer and a dramatist, you knew the world and you knew life. And what a life! That of actors and actresses, of eighteenth-century Venice, of the court of Louis XVI. But you believed in the family, in love and conjugal fidelity, in the dignity of women—in spite of your inate gallantry and your admitted attraction for the 'fair sex'. The women in your plays— wives and widows and daughters—would have blushed to hear the woman I've just quoted.

In your day it was unheard of for the exercise of female

sexuality outside the family to be proclaimed as a right in the name of all women, openly, in front of everyone, without the least reticence. It was unheard of, too, for sin to be considered a pure invention of the authorities, to keep people on a narrow path and take away their freedom.

In your day, even if they sinned, nearly all women admitted that quite apart from ourselves there was a God who—to our advantage, not to his—could give laws to control human behaviour. And how about today? I wonder how many women agree with the idea of this woman deputy. I hope there aren't many, but I don't know: if they were many, it wouldn't mean an advance for the feminist cause but a breakdown of feminity and humanity.

* * *

You've heard the deputy: abortion liberalized and regularized— for the advancement of women.

But will it really be an advance? Enquiries into abortion made by Japanese, English and Hungarian doctors show that, even when they are carried out legally and in specialized nursing homes, abortions are always a danger to the health of the woman, to later child-bearing and further children. Psychologists and psychiatrists say there are other unhappy results; these, they say, may be dozing in the woman's subconscious as a rule, but may appear later in times of crisis.

And this has nothing to do with the moral aspect. Abortion not only violates God's law, but goes against the deepest aspirations of women, disturbing them profoundly.

In many cases it frees not so much the woman as her partner— whether her husband or not—from trouble and worries. It lets him give rein to his sexual desires without taking on the duties connected with them: for women in their relations with men, it is a retrograde step, rather than an advance.

* * *

In the matter of abortion, dear Goldoni, the woman deputy and the feminists have powerful allies today. Some say that regulated abortion is the lesser evil. It prevents back-street abortions and the death of many young women who were once victims of bad practitioners. But the experience of other countries tells us that legalized abortion does not end clandestine abortion. For propaganda purposes the number of victims of clandestine abortions is often made to seem larger than it really is. People say: other civilized countries have legalized abortion; why not Italy? If legalized abortion is a mistake, I retort, why should we have it as well? An illness brought into Italy from outside doesn't become healthy because it's imported; it's still an infection or an epidemic.

* * *

An even more specious argument begins to be heard in defence of abortion: the important thing, people say, is the *twelfth week*.

That is the time when the foetus in the mother's womb has 'two lives'.

The first life is *human*, still vegetal and animal; the second is *humanized*, but humanized on one condition. On condition, that is, that the parents, having just noticed the presence of a small new being, 'call on it to be born', want it, recognize it, make a link of love with it, and thus confer upon it the right to exist. And, it is usually added, the parents must call it. However (a very ugly however), if there's any reason why they should, the parents can, without sin, reject the child and put it away. At most, in order to avoid abuses, and so that it shan't be too easy to put it away, they must listen to doctors or magistrates before deciding.

Alas, dear Goldoni, those 'two lives' exist only in the heads of certain churchmen. Outside their heads, in the mother's womb, in concrete terms, there's just a life sending out an imploring appeal to the parents and to society. People suppose it is up to the parents to create the baby's rights after that *twelfth week*. The opposite is true: it's the child, from the very beginning of its development, that places duties on the parents.

And apart from the baby there's God, who has said: 'Do not kill'. 'Life must be protected with the greatest care from the

moment of conception,' wrote the Second Vatican Council. 'Abortion, like infanticide, is an abominable crime' (GS., n. 51).

*　　*　　*

Dear Goldoni, there are other things to do with the subject, delicate matters I might point out—but let's leave it there. I hope women will manage to achieve new victories, but good ones and elevating ones, to develop what the Lord revealed as the true grandeur of women.

Your plays, dear Goldoni, might give them some help, for they are so full of good sense, filled with girls who are trembling as they wait for married life, of wives who certainly want a happy life and certainly have faults, but who are honest, mindful of their duties, and jealous of their virtue.

Some feminists find all this old fashioned and out of date, trying to make God's laws appear as 'slavery imposed by man'. It means they're choosing non-Christian ways of life.

If I had to recommend a saint to them, it might be Vilgefortis, a woman with an odd name and an even odder life.

She was born in Portugal of pagan parents, and baptized without their knowledge. According to the legend, she made a vow of virginity. Her father promised her in marriage to a King of Sicily, and so she asked God for a miracle to save her. Well, she got one—a thick bristly beard that sprouted on her chin. Naturally the wedding fell through and the girl was freed of her husband, though she was later martyred by her father.

No, I'm not trying to be unkind. Though you might say, lightheartedly, that a bearded saint who's been freed from a husband is just what the feminists could do with when they make fierce suggestions against bearded men.

Come to think of it, Goldoni, you might add a bearded lady to your long cast of women characters!

Andreas Hofer, Tyrolese patriot, born at S. Leonardo in Passiria in 1767 and died (by firing squad) in Mantua in 1810. He led the revolt of the Tyrolean peasants against the Bavarians and the French, whom he defeated on 29 May and 13 August 1809 near Mount Isel. He was later betrayed, taken prisoner by the French and executed on Napoleon's orders. He was not merely a brave partisan but a convinced Christian.

To Andreas Hofer

Dear Hofer,

A month ago, as I passed through Innsbruck, I visited the Hofkirche, a church that was once Franciscan, built in the Renaissance to designs by our own Andrea Crivelli. It was there, on the left of the main door, that I happened to find your tomb. Nearby Joseph Speckbacher and the Capuchin friar Joachim Haspinger, both fellow fighters of yours, are buried too.

You were the innkeeper of San Leonardo in Val Passiria, and you fought two kinds of battle. First, you were a regular soldier in the war against the French in 1796 and 1805; then, as a partisan, you were the leader and the spirit behind the uprising of the Tyrolean people against the Bavarians and the French in 1809. The incredibly brave and able way in which you conducted this guerrilla war aroused the admiration of even Napoleon's generals, and caused the Tyrolean people to take you to their hearts.

Everything began when Montgelas, minister of the Bavarian king, in 1809, without any previous notice or motive, suddenly suppressed all the ceremonies of the Catholic faith: no more processions, no more religious weddings or funerals, no more bell ringing. Montgelas had no idea of the depths of religious feeling in the very Catholic Tyroleans, who respectfully asked the King of Bavaria to have this 'wicked and freedom-killing decree' withdrawn. It was no good, and there was a mass insurrection. The alarm bells rang, echoing from valley to valley, and the peasants came together from every village, some armed with scythes, some with pitchforks, some with old guns: they were dominated by your huge figure, your powerful, decisive voice, your impressive black beard.

The Bavarian army was twice defeated: when tens of thousands of reinforcements were sent by the French and the Saxons your men had to disband and take to guerrilla war.

Then, as happened in the Italian Resistance, you 'took to the mountains'. Two wretches, alas, betrayed you for the usual thirty pieces of silver. Dug out by the French in the hut where you were hiding, you said: 'Do what you like with me, but respect the innocence of my wife and children.' The Viceroy Eugene wanted to pardon you, but Napoleon ordered you to be shot.

Before the execution in Mantua, you blessed your companions kneeling around you, like a patriarch; and you refused to have your eyes bandaged and stood up to face the firing squad. On an open space on the Iselberg, near Innsbruck, they put up a statue to you. On the pedestal is written: *For God, for the Emperor, and for the Fatherland*.

*　　*　　*

Leaving aside the emperor, both inside and outside the Tyrol, I wish your heroism, which was at once gentle and Christian, would inspire people. Let me make myself clear: I don't want a guerrilla war, which I'm sure won't be needed, especially in democratic Italy. But your Christian faith, which was all of a piece, and the close-knit quality of your people, which, with Haspinger, you were able to use in the hour of danger—these I would certainly wish for, with all my heart.

The prophet Elijah said to the people: 'How long halt ye between two opinions? if the Lord be God, follow him: but if Baal, then follow him!' He wanted them to make a serious choice, meaning that you cannot approach God without giving up evil, you cannot waver or fall between two stools.

'Perhaps', 'how' and 'why' weren't the sort of words Tyroleans went in for. There, in the modest inn you ran, people played cards, drank, argued and enjoyed themselves. But when they went back to their homes they had evening prayers with their families, and on Sundays, when they went to Mass, they paused beside the graves of their dead relations in the small cemetery tucked tightly round the church. The atmosphere, the pious traditions, and the leisurely pace of life all encouraged reflection, and reflection developed the conviction which the painter Egger Lienz effectively expressed when he depicted the Tyrolean partisans standing squarely, ready to fight, with Haspinger in front, carrying a crucifix.

We today, swept ahead by the frantic pace of life, lack silence and the chance of reflection. This may be one of the reasons why so many hesitate. Haspinger, a preacher of the old school, who reminds us harshly of the eternal truths, would not be acceptable today. A quieter, more persuasive voice is needed. We cannot bear the great bell tolling on and on; but we may accept a little tinkling household bell.

Brother Candido of the Christian Schools, who lived a century later than you, Hofer, had just this kind of tact. One day he was travelling by train consulting a railway timetable. A boy beside him glanced curiously at the book. 'D'you know this book?' Brother Candido asked. 'You don't? Well, would you like to know what it's used for and how it's used?' Then he explained it all and showed the boy how to work out the timetables and plan the fastest route between one city and another. The boy was interested, tried it out for himself, learnt quickly and thoroughly enjoyed himself. The other passengers followed the conversation with interest and amusement.

At a certain point, without appearing to change the subject, Brother Candido went on: 'Would you like me to show you how to travel on the railway to Heaven?' The boy and the other passengers were amazed. Brother Candido then took an illustrated leaflet out of his travelling bag and explained: 'This is the railway to Heaven. Station of departure: any part of the world. Time of departure: any moment. Time of arrival: the passenger doesn't know. Ticket: being in a state of grace. Ticket collector: examination of conscience. Advice: 1. always have your luggage of good works ready; 2. you can recover your lost luggage through confession, etc.' When he had finished his explanations, he smiled pleasantly and offered the boy and the other passengers the curious, valuable timetable that may, perhaps, have inspired some of them to repentance and new resolutions.

You may say: 'This friar of yours is a very washed-out, small-scale version of my powerful Haspinger.' Well, what can I do about it? In our day, which is religiously weak, suitable means must be found. What matters isn't the method, but whether it's successful in the end: whether it makes people think!

* * *

Even more important is to keep both Catholics and citizens united. We are Christians, but the words of the pagan consul Publius Rutilius apply to us too. He was very fat. One day, to calm down a tremendous fight that showed no sign of ending between two contending parties, he said: 'My friends, as you see I'm very fat and my wife is even fatter. Yet when we agree a small bed is quite big enough for the pair of us. When we quarrel, though, the whole house seems too small to contain us.'

Then I begin to wonder. Rutilius's example will work if there are only two contenders. But in nations and parties today there aren't two quarrelling but dozens, and you can't fit them all in a double bed. Yet if thinking of the common good isn't enough to bring us to unity, fear of the possible damage we may do should make us hold back, at least. Voltaire said: 'Twice I found myself on the edge of ruin: the first time when I lost an argument, the second time when I won it.'

Nations, and political and religious factions, might well take Voltaire's saying to heart. And they should also remember the third man who's always lying in wait: the one who acts as umpire in the quarrel.

Lord Lytton, author of *The Last Days of Pompeii*, wrote: 'A lawyer is a man who, when two people are fighting over an oyster, opens it, sucks out the contents, and gives the shell to the contenders, half each.' That's a little crude, but it's true that always and everywhere our opponent's strength lies in the weakness caused in us by our internal divisions.

These considerations are at least partly suited to the Catholic Church. Its founder, Christ, was afraid of divisions and laid down a strong basis for unity. He said he wanted his followers to be one, to be 'one flock'. To achieve this, he chose twelve from the crowd, and told them that those who heard them would be hearing him. Foreseeing divisions between the twelve and the rest, he made one of them the leader or elder brother, saying to Peter: 'Feed my lambs', 'Confirm your brothers.' So this is the remedy for disunity: if the faithful, priests, religious, and bishops all cling closely to the Pope, no one will break up the Church.

Dear Hofer, your monk Haspinger knew these things, in fact he touched them with his hand. At the time of your Tyrolean insurrection, many bishops, through fear or self-interest, went over to the powerful Napoleon's side. But you in the Tyrol stood up to him and his friends, and sided with Pope Pius VII, who in 1809 excommunicated Napoleon, was arrested by the French, left Rome and went into exile.

These are all things to remember. To put into effect. To put an end to the endless quarrels that exhaust us and scandalize outsiders. To restore the unity of souls, the unity of the Church and of the country. *Fur Gott . . . fur Vaterland . . .* For God and the fatherland, as is written on the Iselberg.

To Jesus

Dear Jesus,

I have been criticized. 'He's a bishop, he's a cardinal,' people have said, 'he's been writing letters to all kinds of people: to Mark Twain, to Péguy, to Casella, to Penelope, to Dickens, to Marlowe, to Goldoni and heaven knows how many others. And not a line to Jesus Christ!'

You know this. With you, I try to keep talking continuously. It's hard to translate this into letters, though: I talk to you about personal things. Such small things, too! And then, what could I write to you, or about you, after all the books that have been written about you?

And then again, we already have the Gospel. As lightning is greater than all fires and radium than all metals, and as the missile flies faster than the poor savage's arrow, so is the Gospel greater than all other books.

All the same, here is my letter. I write it trembling, feeling like a poor deaf mute trying to make himself understood, or like Jeremiah who, when he was asked to preach said to you, very reluctantly, 'Ah, Lord God! behold, I cannot speak: for I am a child'.

* * *

Pilate, presenting you to the people, said: 'Behold the man.' He thought he knew you, but he knew not the least part of your heart, which, a hundred times and in a hundred ways, you showed was tender and merciful.

Your mother. On the cross, you wished not to leave this world without finding a second son to care for her, and you said to John: 'Behold your mother.'

The Apostles. You lived night and day with them, treating them as true friends, bearing with their faults. You taught them with endless patience. The mother of two of them asked for a privileged place for her sons and you told her that it was not

281

honours but suffering they would find with you. Others wanted
the best places too, and you told them to sit in the lowest place,
and serve others.

In the Upper Room you gave them a warning. 'You will be
afraid, you will run away,' you said. They protested; the first to
do so and the most vehement was Peter, who later denied you
three times. You forgave Peter and said to him three times:
'Feed my sheep.'

As for the other Apostles, your forgiveness breaks out above
all in John, Chapter 21. They had been out in a boat all night,
and you were there on the lakeside before dawn, acting as their
cook and servant, lighting the fire, roasting some fish for them
to eat with bread.

Sinners. You are the shepherd who goes in search of the lost
lamb, who is happy to find it again and celebrates when he takes
it back to the flock. You are the good father who, when the
prodigal son returns, flings himself on his neck and embraces
him warmly. On every page of the Gospel you approach sinners,
both men and women, eat at their table, invite yourself in if
they dare not invite you. I have a feeling that you seemed to
worry more about the suffering sin produces in the sinner than
about the offence against God. When you gave them hope of
forgiveness, you seemed to be saying: 'You can't imagine the joy
your conversion gives me!'

* * *

Practical intelligence burned brightly in you, too, as well as this
warmth.

You looked at people's inner life. The faces of the Pharisees
were thin after prolonged religious fasts, and you said you didn't
like them. Their hearts were a very long way from God and it
was the inner life that counted. People must be judged through
their hearts and it was from within, from the hearts of men, that
evil thoughts came: dissoluteness, theft, murder, adultery, lust,
pride, idleness.

You had a horror of useless words. Let your speech be yea,
yea; nay, nay; more than this is derived from evil. When you

pray do not use many words.'

You liked concrete action and reserved behaviour: if you fast, put perfume on your head and wash your face, you told people. If you give alms, do not let your left hand know what your right hand does. To the leper whom you cured you said: tell no man. You told the parents of the girl brought to life very forcefully that they must not go out and proclaim the miracle. You said you were not seeking your own glory, that all you wished was to do the will of your Father.

From the cross, at the end of your life, you said: 'It is finished', but you never wanted to do things by halves. The Apostles told you that the people had been following you for a long time and should be sent away to eat in their own homes; but you said they must be given food where they were. When the meal of multiplied fishes and loaves was over, you told them to gather the fragments, since it was not right for them to go to waste.

You wanted to do good down to the last detail. Having raised Jairus's daughter, you told them to give her something to eat. People said of you: 'He has done all things well.'

* * *

What a light of intelligence poured out from your preaching! Your enemies sent guards from the Temple to arrest you and saw them return empty-handed. When they were asked why they had not brought you, the guards replied: 'No man has ever spoken as he did.' So you enchanted people, who from the very beginning remarked that you spoke with greater authority than the scribes.

Poor scribes! Chained to the six hundred and thirty-four precepts of the law, they used to say that God himself spent a little time every day studying the law and, up there in the sky, studied their dusty old interpretations of it. Whereas you said: 'You have heard that it was said . . . on the contrary I say to you . . .' As master of the law, you claimed the right and the power to perfect it. With magnificent courage you declared that you were greater than the Temple of Solomon. Heaven and earth would pass away, you said, but your words would not pass away.

And you never wearied of instructing people in the synagogues, in the Temple, sitting in the market square or in the fields, walking through the streets, at home, or even at the table.

*   *   *

Today everyone asks for dialogue, and more dialogue. I have counted the dialogues in your Gospel. There are eighty-six: thirty-seven with the disciples, twenty-two with other people, and twenty-seven with your opponents. Today, in teaching, people want group activity based on particular interests. When John the Baptist sent from prison to ask where you were, you wasted no time in chat. Miraculously you healed all the sick who were there and said: 'Go and tell John what you have seen and heard.'

To the Jews of your day, Solomon, David and Jonah were what Dante, Garibaldi and Mazzini are to us. You spoke continually of Solomon, David and Jonah, and of other popular characters. And always with courage.

When you said: 'Blessed are the poor, blessed are the persecuted', I wasn't with you. If I had been, I'd have whispered into your ear: 'For heaven's sake, Lord, change the subject, if you want to keep any followers at all. Don't you know that everyone wants riches and comfort? Cato promised his soldiers the figs of Africa, Caesar promised his the riches of Gaul, and, for better or worse, the soldiers followed them. But you're promising poverty and persecution. Who do you think's going to follow you?' You went ahead unafraid, and I can hear you saying you were the grain of wheat that must die before it bore fruit; and that you must be raised upon a cross and from there draw the whole world up to you.

Today, this has happened: they raised you up on a cross. You took advantage of that to hold out your arms and draw people up to you. And countless people have come to the foot of the cross, to fling themselves into your arms.

*   *   *

Faced with the sight of all these people pouring in for so many centuries, and from every part of the world, to the crucified man, a question arises: were you merely a great and good man, or a God? You gave us the answer yourself, and anyone whose eyes are longing for the light and are not obscured by prejudice accepts it.

When Peter said to you: 'You are the Christ, the son of the living God', you not only accepted this confession, but rewarded it. You always accepted for yourself what the Jews believed belonged to God. They were scandalized when you forgave sins, said you were master of the Sabbath, taught with supreme authority, and declared yourself equal to the Father.

Several times they tried to stone you as a blasphemer, because you said you were God. When at last they took you prisoner and led you to the Sanhedrin, the High Priest asked you solemnly whether you were or were not the son of God. You replied that you were, and that he would see you at the right hand of the Father. Rather than retract this and deny your divinity, you accepted death.

I have written to you, but never have I been so dissatisfied with what I have written as I am this time. I feel I have left out most of what could be said about you, and have said badly what could have been said much better. But there is this comfort: the important thing is not for one person to write about Christ, but for many to love and imitate him.

And happily, in spite of everything, this still happens.